The Essentials of Public Relations

Sam Black

KOGAN
PAGE

First published in 1993
Reprinted 1994

Kogan Page Limited
120 Pentonville Road
London N1 9JN

© Sam Black, 1993

British Library Cataloguing in Publication Data

A CIP record for this book is available from the British Library.

ISBN 0 7494 1083 3

Typeset by Saxon Graphics, Ltd, Derby
Printed and bound in Great Britain by
Biddles Ltd, Guildford and King's Lynn

Contents

List of case histories

List of figures

Preface

The title of this book pleases me for I have long contended that public relations is very simple — it is doing it professionally that is so difficult.

Public relations practice can be described by a number of keywords. It is all about reputation, credibility, confidence, harmony and achieving mutual understanding through truth and full information. These few keywords are the 'essentials' of public relations practice and in this book I will explain how these few simple concepts have developed into a world-wide professional management discipline.

This book includes case histories from different countries which will illustrate public relations in action and emphasize the different ways in which professional public relations advice can promote efficiency and success. Most books that have been written about public relations concentrate on the techniques and skills required, but it is important to remember that for maximum benefit it must be an integral part of the management of the organization and not merely a subsidiary part of marketing.

The practice has come a long way since 1923 when Dr Edward L Bernays wrote the first textbook and delivered the first university course at New York University. It took many years for public relations to become recognized as a professional activity, quite separate from press agentry and publicity. Media relations is still a major part of many programmes but greater benefits accrue when public relations is an integral part of strategic management and is allowed to contribute to the success of an organization in the many different ways which will be described.

Corporate and visual identity is a very important aspect of public relations so this subject is treated in some detail, with examples of some interesting design concepts illustrating how corporate identity pro-grammes have evolved over the years.

It is important to distinguish between public relations which is ubiquitous and the professional practice of public relations which Bernays has described as an art allied to a science. It must be deliberate, planned and sustained and appropriate to the objectives and strategy of the organization on whose behalf it is carried out.

I have lectured on public relations in most countries of the world and it has been most encouraging to see the way in which it has become recognized universally as a positive element in good government and efficient business.

I would like to thank Milner Gray, William Capstick, Danny Moss and a number of other colleagues for their helpful comments and suggestions and my wife, Gwen for her constructive criticism and unfailing encouragement.

Sam Black
June, 1993

1

What is public relations?

The practice of public relations is a management discipline. It is necessary to stress the word 'practice' because this book is about the professional activity as distinct from the overall relationships which exist naturally between individuals and organizations without any help or hindrance from public relations practitioners. Chapter 15 will give a short history of the development of public relations but while this will be of interest, since one can learn much from history, it does not give a clear idea of the present state of the art.

Public relations, as its name implies, concerns the way in which the behaviour and attitudes of individuals, organizations and governments impinge on each other. Attempts to persuade and to mould public opinion are as old as organized society itself, but with the coming of democracy the position changed. When citizens acquired the vote and thus became able to elect governments, the importance of public opinion increased dramatically.

The essence of public relations is the same, whether it is being used in the political arena, the business or commercial field, in community relations, for charities or fund-raising, or in many other situations which each have their special needs. The methods used in these different circumstances will vary considerably and will thus be described separately in the following chapters.

The basic philosophy of public relations practice is very simple. It hypothesizes that with public support and understanding it is much easier to achieve success in attaining identified objectives than in the face of public opposition or indifference. Public relations can be summed up in a few keywords. It is about **reputation, perception, credibility, confidence, harmony**, and **seeking mutual understanding** based on truth and full information. This is not a definition but does indicate the objectives.

Public relations is not confined to the business or commercial fields: it is equally important in government and politics. Vaclav Havel, who became President of Czechoslovakia after the peaceful revolution in November 1989, was interviewed by *Time*, the weekly news magazine, in August 1992 when he resigned following the decision to divide Czechoslovakia into two separate states. Havel emphasized the importance of values not often advanced in world politics – courtesy, good taste, intelligence, decency and, above all, responsibility. These are the same values which are promoted in public relations.

The parameters of public relations

Professional public relations operates in every sphere of business life:

1. Government — national, regional, local and international.
2. Business and industry — small, medium, large and transnational.
3. Community and social affairs.
4. Educational institutions, universities, colleges etc.
5. Hospitals and health care.
6. Charities and good causes.
7. International affairs.

Public relations practice includes the following:

- counselling based on an understanding of human behaviour;
- analysing future trends and predicting their consequences;
- research into public opinion, attitudes and expectations;
- establishing and maintaining two-way communication based on truth and full information;
- preventing conflicts and misunderstandings;
- promoting mutual respect and social responsibility;
- harmonizing the private and the public interest;
- promoting good-will with staff, suppliers and customers;
- improving industrial relations;
- attracting good personnel and reducing labour turnover;
- promotion of products or services;
- projecting a corporate identity.

This is a formidable list, but it emphasizes the fact that public relations is an integral part of almost every aspect of organization or management.

The public relations hexagon

One way of describing the role of public relations is by considering the hexagon model (Figure 1.1). The six sides of the hexagon represent the different factors which influence the role and scope of public relations.

The iceberg syndrome

The iceberg syndrome (see Figure 1.2) has been drawn to illustrate the contrast between many people's perception of public relations practice and the very complex reality.

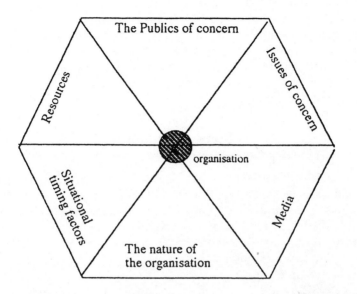

Figure 1.1 *The public relations hexagon*

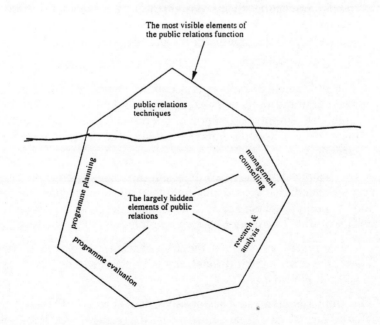

Figure 1.2 *The iceberg syndrome*

This iceberg model tends to be characteristic of organizations in which public relations is practised mainly as a reactive function. In such bodies, public relations tends to have little, if any, input into strategic decision making. Organizations which may have hitherto adopted a narrow reactive approach to the public relations function are increasingly realizing that a more proactive approach will be of direct benefit in coping with the changing environment of business.

Some definitions

It is very difficult to define public relations practice and most, if not all definitions are descriptions of the effect of public relations rather than true definitions. The Institute of Public Relations amended its definition in November 1987 as follows: 'public relations practice is the planned and sustained effort to establish and maintain goodwill and mutual understanding between an organization and its publics'.

A more comprehensive definition is the Mexican Statement signed in August 1978 by representatives of more than 30 national and regional public relations associations. This stated:

> Public relations practice is the art and social science of analyzing trends, predicting their consequences, counselling organization's leadership and implementing planned programmes of action which will serve both the organization's and the public interest.

A good definition is given in the *Webster New International Dictionary*:

> The promotion of rapport and goodwill between a person, firm or institution and other persons, special publics, or the community at large, through the distribution of interpretative material, the development of neighbourly interchange and the assessment of public reaction.

A few simple definitions worth noting are: good performance, publicly acknowledged; doing good and getting credit for it; reconciling the private and the public interest; acting as a bridge between an organization and the outside world. The author prefers a simple but comprehensive definition:

> Public relations practice is the art and science of achieving harmony with the environment through mutual understanding based on truth and full information.

The emphasis on art and science may be a surprise. The quotation from Charles Zeanah (see Figure 1.3) explains the science label. The art lies in the need and opportunity to use ideas, imagination and creativity in planning public relations programmes.

PUBLIC RELATIONS...is not anything that a company or an institution or an organization does. Rather it is the result of what is accomplished because public relations is what goes on in the minds of people. Every action by an individual or a group has a way of affecting public opinion, favourably or unfavourably. The most important fundamental in the practice of public relations is the attitude of the mind. It is partly a philosophy, or perspective, in thinking about things. In essence, the products of public relations work of value are the end reactions that motivate people to make a purchase or to believe in something or someone. The result can be attributed to a rare combination of specialized skills and a correct judgment. In this regard, I perceive public relations as an art. Further, I propose that public relations also is a science since it can be properly oriented to a set of objectives or a statement of purpose. As in the sciences, public relations incorporates the analysis of a problem with the development of a method for its solution. Public relations thus becomes the unique know-how of getting things done successfully. It is a keen sensitivity to people and timing in terms of markets, competitors, community crises or world affairs.

Figure 1.3 *An American corporate view — a perception, by Charles H Zeanah APR*

It is important to realize that there are two distinct branches of public relations practice. The first and obvious sector is the reactive part — reacting to problems, dealing with crises and managing change. This includes protection of reputation. The other half of the work is quite different but equally important. It is usually referred to as the *proactive sector* of public relations. The Mexican Statement refers to it as: 'implementing planned programmes of action which will serve both the organization's and the public interest'. This includes counselling which may be very important. It is highly desirable that public relations considerations should be taken into account when planning corporate strategy and policy.

Public relations is the responsibility of the decision makers. Only if top management rightly appreciates the importance of this activity can it make its maximum contribution to efficiency and profitability. It is no coincidence that most of the successful national and international companies devote considerable attention to their public relations programmes.

Sir John Harvey-Jones summed it up succinctly in *The Economist* (16 March 1989). He stated that the main activities with which a company chairman should concern himself are strategic planning and public relations. The company chairman, or chief executive should take a personal interest in the organization's public relations but will usually delegate responsibility to a board member or departmental head. The person in charge of public relations need not be a member of the board but should be regarded as a member of the management team and should have direct and easy access to top management.

A medium size or large organization has a choice between having its own public relations staff or using the services of outside public relations consultants. Some companies use a combination of these two methods, bringing in consultants to deal with overload of work or special assignments. Each organization must assess its own needs and decide on the most appropriate method of meeting its public relations requirements. The following Checklist may be useful to companies without previous experience.

Checklist

How does your organization measure up?

1. Do you have an overall public relations policy?
2. Does your public relations department or public relations consultants report at a level high enough to make an impact on management policy?
3. Do you fear the media and keep them at arm's length or enlist their interest in your activities?
4. Is the budget for public relations adequate to meet routine needs with additional funding readily available for special requirements?
5. Are your telephone and reception staff well informed and always courteous?
6. Are your premises easy to find and well maintained?
7. Do you have a consistent and well designed house style, including logo, house colour and typographical style?
8. Is your Annual Report and Accounts a credit to your company and used to secure media attention and good general publicity?
9. Do internal communications receive the attention they need?
10. What attention is given to community relations and corporate social responsibility?

Seven deadly sins of public relations

It is possible to sum up some of the worst failings of ineffective public relations programmes under the following headings:

■ **Functional myopia**: Failure to appreciate the full scope of the important contribution public relations can make to good management.

- **Faucet philosophy**: We will turn on public relations when we need it.
- **Putting the cart before the horse**: Who needs research?
- **Local anaesthesia**: Let's handle this on the local level.
- **Good news neurasthenia**: We believe in full and complete public information so long as it is positive and reflects favourably upon us.
- **The one-shot communication tic**: Why do you accuse us of not communicating? — it was mentioned in our last annual report.
- **The shadow delusion**: The low profile philosophy. This aberration is based on the belief that an organization can make itself invisible when it chooses.

(This is based on a chapter in *The Power of Public Relations* by Joseph F Awad, Praeger, 1985).

2
Strategic public relations, corporate and public affairs

It has been stressed in the last chapter that public relations practice is a management discipline and should play a part in strategic and corporate planning.

Strategic management differentiates between shortly, medium- and long-term considerations and the strategic indications are likely to be different in each case. Strategic management concerns an organization as a whole and how it can adapt effectively to constantly changing circumstances.

It is perhaps useful to distinguish between strategy and tactics. Strategy can be regarded as long-term planning, while tactics are more action oriented and tend to be short term in effect. This is not universally true, however, as strategy may also be short term and in practice the distinction is less formal, requiring an organization to be flexible in its corporate policy. Strategic decisions are those which determine the direction of an enterprise and its ultimate viability in the light of the predictable, the unpredictable and unknown changes that might occur in the surrounding environment.

The strategic role of public relations

Professor Henry Mintzberg has suggested five possible interpretations of strategy — the five Ps:

1. As a Plan — some conscious intended course of action.
2. As a Ploy — a manoeuvre intended to outwit an opponent.
3. As a Pattern — a specific stream of actions directed towards an end — here two forms of strategy may be identified: *emergent* and *deliberate*.
4. As a Position — a means of locating an organization in its environment — strategy is the mediating force between the organization and its environment.

5. As a Perspective — here strategy is a means of looking inside an organization; the way in which managements perceive their world and competitive environment — the accepted recipe for success.

In practice, these five Ps have to be integrated into an overarching strategic policy. The role of public relations is thus to reconcile these various considerations in a manner which will satisfactorily integrate external factors with internal policies.

Public relations practitioners often think of strategy in terms of a set of activities designed to generate goodwill and publicity — in this sense their approach is to treat strategy as a series of 'ploys'. If public relations is to contribute to the formation and achievement of the corporate mission and objectives, it must be concerned more with strategy as both a position and a perspective. In other words, it is necessary to seek to reconcile management's internal vision and values with the organization's external position. Both of these must reflect prevailing and likely future environmental pressures. Thus as a strategic function, public relations must be concerned with managing the relationships between an organization and its environment — or more specifically its relationships with both external and internal key strategic constituencies. Put another way, public relations has a strategic role of bridging the gap between an organization's internal perspective and its external positioning. This is illustrated in Figure 2.1.

The conventional view of an organization constantly changing in response to its environment is unlikely to be true in many instances. Most companies have a corporate strategy which favours stability and which has an in-built characteristic opposition to change. When change does occur, it is the responsibility of public relations to explain the significance of the new conditions by integrated communication which uses many different messages but all coordinated for maximum effect.

Management by objectives describes the most usual style in favour at present, but other management styles have their adherents:

- management by charisma;
- management by default;
- management by walk about;
- management by accident;
- management by consent.

The style of management that best describes the public relations inspired style can perhaps be called 'management by consent'. All organizations must be sensitive to future trends and aware of their possible repercussions on the future of the company. Sometimes this is called 'environmental scanning' or 'futurism' but issues management is a better term as it implies that the company does not merely monitor change but plans to take it into continuing consideration in planning corporate strategy. Two

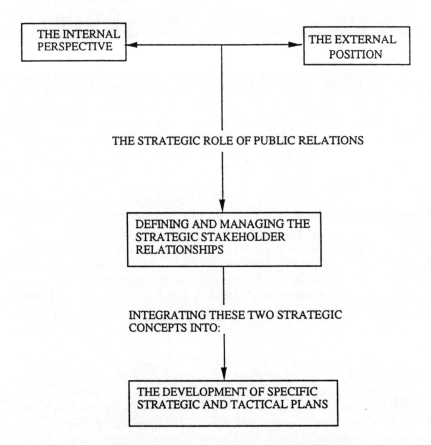

Figure 2.1 *The strategic role of public relations*

quotations are relevant here: 'issues are unsolved problems' and 'an issue is merely a trend whose time has come'. The Conference Board of America has defined an issue as 'a condition or pressure, either internal or external, that, if it continues, will have a significant effect on the functioning of the organization or its future interest.'

Current management theory regards organizations as comprising linked coalitions, with decisions and agreed objectives determined largely by relative power and influence. There are many sources of power in an organization and in many of these public relations advice can be valuable. The following list of sources of power in a typical organization emphasizes this point:

■ formal authority;
■ control of scarce resources;
■ organizational structures and procedures;
■ control of decision processes;

- boundary management;
- control of information;
- management of change;
- control of technology;
- alliances and informal networks;
- countervailing power;
- symbolism and the meaning of language;
- gender power.

The effects of these internal power confrontations are tempered by the effect of external power sources such as customers, suppliers and the community.

Cliff Bowman, in *The Essence of Strategic Management* (Prentice Hall) explains that strategic management implies that policy decisions will be made only after a great deal of information gathering, analysis and forecasting. The mission statement which has become so popular, is seen by some management experts as the first stage in strategic planning, while others criticise it as an alternative to corporate policy.

Mission statements, and the Japanese messages of 'strategic intent' are only meaningless words unless they are the basis of specific policies and strategies. This is where wise public relations counsel can be invaluable. Mission statements are excellent initiatives, but only if they are true reflections of top management thinking and are revised from time to time in the light of environmental change or organizational necessity. Bowman stresses that value from a mission statement comes firstly from the processes management has to go through in drawing one up. To meet the criteria listed in such a statement, management has to address all the fundamental strategic issues.

It is difficult to understand why there has been some cynical comments about the usefulness of published mission statements. It has even been suggested that an organization should publish its formal statement of values separately from any mission statement.

Corporate relations and public affairs

The early development of public relations in the USA was mainly in the corporate field and it was only later that its use spread to non-profit areas. In the UK, the initial developments were mainly in the government sector: corporate acceptance of public relations practice came later. Nowadays, of course, the acceptance of public relations has spread right across the spectrum.

A classic concept of public relations in the US corporate sector was the attempt by an organization to influence or change society to create a climate in which the organization could pursue its objectives without interference. This aspect of public relations is correctly termed 'public affairs'. Unfortunately, this term appears to have a better appeal to some companies, particularly in the US, than the correct generic term 'public relations'. Used correctly, the term public affairs covers relations with governmental, statutory and other official bodies and thus embraces a much narrower concept than the comprehensive function of public relations as delineated in Chapter 1.

As Shakespeare said: 'what's in a name?' An American commented:

> 'My name is public relations. But you can call me communications, or you can call me public affairs, or you can call me public information, or corporate relations, or issues management, or publicity, or marketing communication . . . so long as you leave me to get on with my job.'

It is rather surprising that as practitioners achieve seniority in their companies, their title often changes from public relations to public affairs. The logic of this is difficult to comprehend. The tragedy of this multiplicity of terms is that it hinders the true understanding of the professional practice of public relations. Another unfortunate practice is the tendency to refer to public relations as 'PR'. This bad habit is encouraged by many practitioners who are too lazy to use the correct title.

The value of case histories

The study of case histories is an excellent way of appreciating the wide range of situations which need public relations attention and the even wider field of opportunity for public relations to play a creative part in the success of every kind of organization. For this reason, this book includes a number of case histories from the UK and other countries which illustrate the disparate nature of the function.

Most of these case histories have won awards in competitions and the practitioners concerned have won the approbation of their peers. These reports have been called case histories, rather than case studies, because they report the nature of the problem or opportunity and the way in which it was tackled, successfully in most instances. A case *study*, on the other hand, should be a much more exhaustive analysis of the background and a detailed analytical study of the way in which the programme was carried out.

Some of these case histories encompass several different areas of public relations and so they may not appear in the obvious chapter. The list of case histories which follows the contents page will make it possible to trace any particular item.

Case history 1
Financial implications of a radical name and brand change

During 1991, Trusthouse Forte reached a critical juncture in its development with the launch of a new branding structure and change of name to Forte. The company considered it was important to demonstrate to City audiences, principally shareholders, analysts and the media, that the repositioning of the group would contribute to increased profits and shareholder value.

Shareholder approval was required for the name change, so informed and favourable comment was needed from the leisure analysts who follow the fortunes of the company. Furthermore, favourable comment on the new corporate identity was desirable from the press who are often cynical on this subject.

Research
Forte has a structured investor relations programme dividing analysts and institutions into sub-categories of importance and influence. It seeks to deliver a predetermined level of contact and information and collects feedback which is stored on a central database. This comprehensive picture of key City attitudes is supplemented by annual participation in the MORI survey of City opinion and *ad hoc* research carried out by UBS Phillips & Drew and Brunswick Public Relations.

The research was used when formulating the strategic business plan and branding philosophy. It showed that institutions had a low awareness of the range and choice of the Group's portfolio. They focused principally on the most prominent hotels and had little knowledge of the restaurant interests.

In addition, the research helped to identify areas of concern which could be addressed in the communication plan. This element of the work was supplemented by desk research to identify the strengths and weaknesses of recent corporate identity launches by other companies. As well as providing lessons for the Forte launch, it identified which journalists were sceptics on the subject and which were sympathetic.

Planning
The primary objective was to ensure the most visible aspect of the rebranding, the proposed name change, was well received but that this high profile issue did not obscure the clear business rationale behind the change.

The second objective was to capitalize fully on the opportunity provided by the rebranding to change perceptions of THF and to confirm the strengths and opportunities for growth in the 90s and beyond. The planning faced two specific constraints. Approval had to be sought from the shareholders so the launch timetable was dictated by the notice period for the AGM. Secondly, the cohesion of the programme was difficult to understand without visual examples, eg re-signed hotels, but it was difficult to produce these without breaching confidentiality.

The main challenge, therefore, was to develop corporate materials which would illustrate and explain the rebranding and new identity, before it actually existed physically. At the same time, an extensive list of possible issues and questions was drawn up so that they could be addressed in the communications.

The key messages which needed to form the basis of all communications were agreed as the following:

- the diversity and choice offered by the Group;
- the strong brands in hotels and catering;
- the unique breadth of the hotels portfolio;
- international presence;
- the Group positioned for growth in an expanding international market.

Implementation

The programme consisted of four phases: the planning, the corporate and brand launch, the AGM and demonstrating the changes. There were three key elements to the work during the planning phase:

1. Creating a receptive climate. Knowledge of the proposed rebranding of the hotel portfolio was widespread, so the public relations work in 1991 was designed to guide the target audiences towards the logic of what would be announced, without revealing too much, thus losing the impact of the launch. The results announcement in April was used to guide City opinion and confirm the launch date of June, thus creating a sense of excitement.
2. A contingency plan to cope with a leak was prepared. About 250 people inside and outside the company were working on various aspects of the project in the run-up to the announcement. Fortunately no leak occurred.
3. Much of the time in Phase 1 was devoted to the preparation of materials for the launches.

In the early stages, it was necessary to brief certain individuals on a confidential basis before any of the main marketing materials were available. An exhibition was constructed using prototype signs and a series of easily portable panels telling the story of the rebranding, describing its implementation for each part of the business and providing mock ups of items as diverse as menus, stationery and signage to illustrate the visual impact and the linkage between brands and collections.

A circular had to be sent to shareholders to inform them of the proposed name change and to seek their approval at the AGM. It was decided that the circular should be visually exciting so that it could be used as a key document to inform a wide range of interested parties.

A fact file was put together which gave at a glance a summary of key facts and figures about the company and its operations and incorporating the rebranding.

An audio-visual presentation was prepared to convey the visual style and effectiveness of the rebranding and to give an impression of its impact once implemented.

A news release was prepared which summarized the main elements of the announcement in a series of bullet points, backed up by more details.

Corporate and brand launch

The City communications programme was coordinated with other communication programmes, particularly those to the staff in the UK and overseas.

Analysts were identified as a key group since they would influence initial media comment and long-term investor sentiment. A major presentation was given to them on the morning of the announcement. This included an exhibition illustrating the rebranding, an audio-visual presentation and a presentation by chief executive, Rocco Forte, followed by a question and answer session. The circular to shareholders was posted on the same day so that shareholders would receive it the next morning, to coincide with comment on the rebranding in their newspapers.

The AGM

In the weeks leading up to the announcement on 8 May and the AGM on 4 June, a programme of meetings and dinners was arranged with the aim of seeing shareholders accounting for at least 50 per cent of votes. Reactions and voting intentions were carefully monitored. This helped to create a climate of understanding which resulted in an unusually high percentage of shares being voted in support of the name change, by proxy, ahead of the AGM.

A special video which had to be shot in four weeks, was made for the AGM, following the announcement. It was a difficult brief, to raise enthusiasm without seeming to take the vote for granted. The vote of confidence from institutions helped to reassure shareholders to vote in favour, resulting in an overwhelming 98 per cent result supporting the name change.

With the vote secured at the AGM, the next priority was to show the name change working. The public relations campaign continued but changed tactics to look for in-depth coverage of the business logic now the initial tone was set. This dictated a smaller number of targets willing to devote more space. The answer was to achieve a leading article in each specialist field. The response was excellent. This phase was supported by major corporate advertising to impress the City. This campaign won critical acclaim.

Shareholders were given a forecast of the rebranding by including a complete redesign of the annual report. Hotel visits in each brand were organized for analysts and the top 100 shareholders.

Evaluation

The first objective was to gain positive coverage in the main financial pages and to avoid negative pieces in the tabloids. This objective was achieved. The reaction of analysts was positive and the share price was steady.

The next test of support was the AGM and the success achieved here surpassed all expectations. A MORI research study was undertaken once the vote was through. Understanding was firmest among the priority audiences targeted. Results from analysts noted a strong correlation between their view of the benefits of the rebranding and the initial objectives. There was significant support from institutions.

A formidable public relations challenge had been tackled positively with very satisfactory results.

Budget

As far as possible, the communication costs were built into the on-going investor relations programme. The principal additional costs were:

Exhibition materials and audio-visual presentations	£25,000
Circular to shareholders	£70,000
Roadshow to institutions	£3,000
	a total of £98,000

Comment

This case history by Forte plc, together with their entry in the Internal Communications section (see Chapter 10) won the prestigious 1992 Sword of Excellence award offered each year by the Institute of Public Relations for the best public relations programme. The chairman of the judges, John Garnett, commented that Forte plc had shown that excellence is a matter of winning the hearts and minds of all employees in the enterprise. Forte were also successful in convincing the City that repositioning the group would increase profits and shareholder value.

Case history 2
Explaining the Wirral Hospital NHS Trust

The story of a public relations campaign that comprised community relations, employee relations, media relations and parliamentary lobbying.

The situation

In October 1990, the chief executive, Frank Burns and the management of the Wirral Hospital were concerned that their decision to apply for first wave Trust status might not be fully understood either by their own staff or by the people in the Wirral's 140,000 households who provide the majority of the hospital's patients.

The concept of Trust status was under fire in the media, nationally and locally, with strong criticism that Trust status was an 'opting-out' process fraught with operational and financial problems. Within the hospital, staff at all levels had expressed opposition to the Trust application.

The brief given to a small public relations consultancy, Kenyon Associates, was to make the people of Wirral aware of the change of status of their hospital in April 1991, explaining the reasons for applying for Trust status and showing the benefits that Trust status was bringing. The 4500 members of staff at the two-site hospital were also to be addressed by an awareness campaign, with special emphasis on their particular concerns and need for information.

As the programme developed, it also became necessary to play a part in lobbying Government for funding. A diversion was the need to meet media interest in a succession of tragic incidents.

Planning

The Hospital Management decided to inform the community and staff fully through a media relations programme, backed up by internal publications, a specially commissioned video, and a limited amount of literature for external circulation. It was realized that entrenched opinions about Trust status would not be changed easily, so the aim was simply to put the case for Trust status and to promote understanding of the consequent changes. The programme expanded later to include promoting the hospital as a centre of excellence in patient care.

The budget for the programme was flexible as it was difficult to forecast the necessary expenditure. The overriding consideration in making expenditure decisions was that this was NHS money: any suggestion that money was being wasted when it could have been spent on better services or facilities would have undermined the whole programme.

Implementation

Kenyon Associates had already established good links with the hospital management at a senior level, and had less extensive contact with the work-force in the wards. Briefing sessions with the Chief Executive and his senior officers established the philosophy of the programme, while an effective system for day-to-day communications was devised.

Both management and staff were keen that as much news as possible should be sent out. Fortunately, the Wirral is served by two daily regional newspapers and by two long-established 'free' papers which cover nearly the whole of the hospital's patient catchment area. There are also two local radio stations, BBC Merseyside and Radio City, as well as Granada and BBC news teams operating in the area. It was decided to use the local media widely to state the case for Trust status, winning coverage for items about the progress of the application and the projected benefits that would result. Negative comment was countered by positive news items.

A supplement in one of the local newspapers, circulated to every household, was produced during the run-up to consideration of the Trust application, with supporting arguments clearly stated. The hospital's staff magazine, *Insite*, also used to keep employees informed about progress of the application and a small brochure was produced for distribution at GPs' surgeries.

A video was commissioned which explained the background to the Trust application, emphasizing continuity and other benefits. The video was designed for use at public meetings and within the hospital. An exhibition stand was also produced for similar use.

Once the decision was made to confer Trust status, the emphasis changed from basic information to communicating the expected benefits of the imminent new status.

The run-up to Trust status

Positive messages were now sent to the media about the forthcoming changes and the improvements in service from the hospital.

Plans were prepared to mark 'Trust Day' with informal and low-key celebrations. Babies born on 1 April received gifts from the Trust chairman, and a range of T-shirts and hats were on sale for the benefit of the hospital's League of Friends. The low-key approach was adopted as it was felt that too much emphasis on the change might confuse patients.

The national anti-Trust campaign was now at its height, with daily stories about hospitals going 'private' and facing potential financial difficulties. It was this attack on the Trust principle that decided the hospital to continue to emphasize the advantages in the next stage of the programme.

The first year

What started as a fairly limited media relations and local information programme widened out into a number of new public relations initiatives.

The hospital had applied to the Government for a £8.3 million grant to be made available for the redevelopment of one of the hospital sites and the provision of improved services. Kenyon Associates were commissioned, at short notice, to produce a video to support this application. When the successful outcome of this application was known it was a major local media item.

The scope of the public relations activities widened. The Trust's annual report was voted the best NHS Trust report in the Annual King's Fund National Association of Health Services and Trusts awards. A newsletter was produced for GPs to keep them informed of developments. Briefings were also produced for local councillors.

In the middle of all this activity, there were three incidents at the hospital involving the death of patients through 'lack of care'. This unprecedented series of accidents made national news and some people tried to blame this on the Trust concept. It was very difficult to stop negative comment but after it had passed, the Hospital Management felt that the 'damage limitation' exercise that took place was as effective as it could be in such difficult circumstances.

The budget

The total budget, including fees, was £43,825 in 15 months, out of a total hospital budget of £60 million. The major cost items were the production of the videos, newsletters, magazines, posters, annual report and the exhibition stand.

The results

The hospital was named in the *Independent on Sunday* as one the country's favourite 12 hospitals, according to a patient survey.

Media awareness of the new status is extensive: the hospital is now almost invariably referred to as the 'Wirral Hospital' or 'the Trust', rather than by its old names Arrowe Park and Clatterbridge. Management believes this is a crucial point in presenting the hospital as a unified organization.

Emphasis on the hospital's points of excellence has helped to boost staff morale, according to managers in direct contact with staff. This is demonstrated also by the increased number of contributions by staff to their magazine.

There were some ethical constraints as considerations of patient care came first at all times. There were occasions when good stories or projects had to be abandoned or suspended for medical or ethical reasons.

Comment
This case history is a very good example of how a successful public relations programme can be planned and implemented under very difficult circumstances by a small consultancy working closely with the client and with a limited budget.

Case history 3
The death and life of a company — Treats Ice Cream

This is the story of how BRAHM Public Relations was central to the achievement of the business aim — the survival of the firm.

The crisis began on 10 January 1991, when Birds Eye Walls announced the closure of its Leeds-based subsidiary Treats Ice Cream with the loss of over 350 jobs. They stated that they deeply regretted having to close the business but that the decision was unavoidable.

Although BRAHM were consultants to the company they only had a few days' notice of the closure plan. As part of the existing public relations programme, a crisis public relations strategy had been established for Treats, but no one could have foreseen the final crisis of Treats, a successful company, facing imminent closure. Nevertheless, the existing crisis plan served as a framework for identifying relevant target audiences and the best ways of reaching them. Added to the target audience list were the potential decision makers in this campaign — the boards of Birds Eye Walls, the parent company Unilever and Unilever shareholders.

The consultancy identified a range of major objections to be raised against the closure plan. Key points included the job losses, the local economic, social and community effects, Treats' role in the UK ice cream market and the national interest in relation to European competition.

The local and national media campaign emphasized that here was a successful company having to close. This brought into question the motives of those behind the closure and concern over their reluctance to consider a management buy-out.

Public pressure was maintained by a regular flow of news stories to keep the problem in the foreground. Coordinated lobbying was undertaken by Treats' customers, MPs, the Council, the Church, the trade union and employees. Points of concern were raised with Birds Eye Walls and Unilever.

The necessity for the third stage of the campaign was preempted by the announcement of the acceptance of the buy-out offer. If necessary, it would have sought to exert more explicit and direct pressure on Birds Eye Walls and Unilever.

The aftermath

A series of post-announcement activities were undertaken to highlight Treats' positive image. To thank the parties involved in saving the company, a party was held for journalists and a civic reception for all the key opinion formers. A book describing the successful campaign to save Treats was issued to a wide range of audiences. The Bishop of Leeds performed a blessing on the building site of the new factory for the company.

Evaluation

The objective to save the company and ensure a future for its management, work-force and customers was achieved. A new £5 million facility for the company is in hand to ensure its position as one of the leaders in its market.

Initially, there was considerable doubt about the possibility of success. As one manager at Treats despaired at the outset, 'Once they (Unilever) make up their mind, that's it. They've made unpopular decisions in the past and stuck to their guns despite the flak they were getting'.

An editorial in the *Yorkshire Evening Post* of 25 January 1991 praised the campaign and described it as a model of its kind. Denis Healey, MP described the public relations as 'excellent'.

The budget

The cost of the campaign was undertaken within the consultancy's normal retainer fee of £2500 per month.

Comment

Even large companies can be made to see the error of their proposals if local opposition is mobilized and professionally directed.

Case history 4
Keep Hillingdon whole

The following is a good example of a local authority calling in a public relations consultancy to help it overturn an unwelcome proposal of the Local Government Boundary Commission.

Objective

The Local Government Boundary Commission proposed, as part of its review of council boundaries, that all of Heathrow Airport and five villages to the north of the airport should be transferred to the London Borough of Hounslow.

Hillingdon Council wished to retain the villages in line with residents' views and to incorporate the 30 per cent of Heathrow Airport not within its boundaries in the interests of the efficient provision of council services.

Dewe Rogerson was appointed to help Hillingdon Council to overturn the Commission's draft proposals.

Background

The Boundary Commission, in its draft recommendations, took as its base two major factors. Firstly, the view that those properties affected by airport related noise should be administered by the same local authority that had responsibility for the airport; and secondly, that the villages to the north of the airport (between the M4 and A4) had a greater affinity with Hounslow than Hillingdon.

Strategy

It was decided that, while the two issues needed to be tackled separately, there needed to be a common theme linking the two arguments. The rationale for this was that the 'villages' issue would generate considerable public support while the 'airport' issue would not. Linking the two themes brought vicarious public support to the airport element of the campaign.

At the same time, it was necessary to produce a comprehensive submission to the Commission responding to all the issues raised in order to justify a change of mind.

The action stage

The strategy adopted resulted in two distinct communication programmes:

1. The campaign for the villages

To provide a focus for public support, the KEEP HILLINGDON WHOLE campaign was devised jointly and a campaign logo developed for use on leaflets, posters, letterheads and in the media. Care was taken to ensure that the campaign complied with the requirements of the Local Government Code of Practice on Publicity.

Following a review of the criteria used by the Commission to assess boundary changes, it was agreed that, while the local population were known to be against the proposed move to Hounslow, this opposition needed to be quantified and explained.

A detailed opinion poll of residents' views was conducted. To ensure that the results were not influenced by the debate on the boundary review, the questionnaire was devised in such a way that those responding were not aware of the reasons for the poll until the last few questions.

Local residents were encouraged to make their comments known to the Commission through a leaflet and poster campaign and to copy their letters to the local authority.

Meetings were also held with local representatives and residents' groups to discuss their views on the proposals, explain the process and how views could be made known to the Commission.

In addition, other service providers in the borough were invited to support the Hillingdon campaign. The Health Authority, the local Family Practitioners Committee, the Magistrates Courts Committee, local schools and others put very persuasive arguments to the Commission in support of the Hillingdon line.

2. The campaign for the airport

The campaign to bring all of Heathrow Airport into the borough did not generate much public interest. The bulk of the airport (70 per cent) was already in Hillingdon, including most of the terminal capacity and Hillingdon had a proven track record in the provision of services to the airport.

It was decided to major on this aspect, promoting the 'centre of excellence' argument and the disruption which would be caused should responsibility be transferred. Equally, even if Heathrow were to be transferred to Hounslow, Hillingdon would still have to provide some of the existing services, such as emergency planning, because of the second borough airport at RAF Northolt. Again, a coalition of support was sought for the case, by briefing the major airport operators, together with Heathrow Airport Limited and London Transport.

Considerable efforts were exerted to marshal the best arguments for keeping the airport in Hillingdon. A database of statistics was developed to back up the level of expertise and to evaluate the strongest arguments.

The Commission had accepted the principle of Heathrow being in one borough but had chosen Hounslow because:

a)   more people in Hounslow were affected by airport noise;
b)   more Hounslow residents were employed at the airport.

Hillingdon's formal submission addressed these points with persuasive counter arguments.

In response to the first point, it was emphasized that the airport noise affected residents of a much wider area, including Slough, Richmond, Windsor etc. If the logic of the Commission was that the local authority which administered the airport should also be responsible for all those people affected by aircraft noise, then the borough boundaries throughout all of Western London, and a substantial part of the Home Counties should be changed. This is obviously not possible, nor indeed, desirable.

A noise contour map was produced which highlighted the fact that Hillingdon residents were affected by the loudest noise generated by aircraft on the ground. Hillingdon had also developed a sophisticated noise measurement facility at the airport. It was important to promote and explain the nature of, and reasons for its development.

The question of Hounslow residents employed at the airport was tackled by approaching the major employers, BAA and British Airways, to obtain Heathrow employee survey data. This showed that, while Hounslow had the largest proportion of airport workers as residents, the figure was only marginally (3 per cent) more than those who were residents of Hillingdon and that the trend was a decline in Hounslow based employees while the Hillingdon figures were rising steadily.

In addition, a number of other interests whose work was affected by the airport were briefed on the Commission proposals and encouraged to submit their views. The local MP and MEP were also kept informed.

The measurement stage
The results of the opinion research showed that local people had a strong affinity with Hillingdon and felt alienated and isolated from Hounslow. This was borne out by answers about shopping habits, use of public transport and local services. Response to the proposed move to Hounslow showed only 3 per cent in favour with an overwhelming 85 per cent against.

The research findings formed an integral part of Hillingdon's submission. In addition, the Commission received about 600 representations from individuals including residents from the Hillingdon villages. The arguments promoted mirrored those promoted by Hillingdon: established communities; strong affinity with Hillingdon; and good links with North Hillingdon.

Airport users and other commercial interests all confirmed the need for the whole of Heathrow to be located in one authority. In addition, there was support for Hillingdon from Heathrow Airport Limited, British Airways, Hillingdon Health Authority and Hillingdon Area Magistrates Courts Committee.

The Commission concluded in its further draft proposals in January 1992 that there was:

- strong opposition from residents; and
- a higher level of expertise and experience in Hillingdon in providing services to the satisfaction of users and operators of the airport.

Consequently, the Commission concluded that Heathrow should be united in Hillingdon.

The next stage was a final consultative period which closed on 13 April 1992. Hillingdon submitted further evidence, this time supporting the Commission's revised proposals.

Costs
The campaign had been running for about 18 months. It is difficult to assess the exact costs because Hillingdon's own resources were used wherever possible. The research project cost about £10,000 and consultancy fees were £24,000 per annum.

Conclusion
The Commission's initial proposal has been successfully overturned and the revised proposals met all Hillingdon's objectives. The final decision on the new boundaries was made by the Secretary of State in early 1993. Hillingdon thus achieved all its objectives.

Comment
Good, well presented arguments can sometimes persuade even an official commission to change its recommendations.

Case history 5
Combating environmental restraints in Canada

In these days of concern with environmental factors, an attempt to drill for oil off Canada's shores was bound to arouse strong opposition from many directions, particularly from the fishermen.

About two years earlier, Texaco Canada had failed to secure planning permission to drill. LASMO plc, a smaller oil company, decided to try its luck and started by taking advice from a local public relations company.

Introduction
In mid-1989, LASMO plc, an international oil company with its head office in London, in partnership with a Crown corporation of the Province of Nova

Scotia, agreed to pursue development of two offshore oil deposits, Cohasset and Panuke, located about 250 km south east of Halifax, Nova Scotia.

Months earlier, the Exxon Valdez had run aground off Alaska and 15 months earlier the governments of Nova Scotia and Canada had agreed to a moratorium on drilling on George's Bank, located less than 500 nautical km from the Cohasset and Panuke fields, thwarting an ambitious exploration programme planned by Texaco Canada.

A local public relations company, McArthur, Thompson & Law was retained to work with LASMO Nova Scotia Limited to build a better understanding with target audiences as a means of avoiding conflict about the proposed project. The plan was to win regulatory approval by autumn 1990.

Research

Based on the unhappy experience of Texaco Canada, it was realized that LASMO's success would depend, in large part, on satisfying the concerns of the fishermen and the environmentalists. The spring 1989 edition of the *Decima Quarterly*, published a survey of Canadian public opinion by one of Canada's foremost research organizations, which reported that the environment was the top concern among Canadians. Respondents believed that government involvement in environmental issues was necessary and over one-third had little confidence in oil companies.

In order to assess the underlying problems facing LASMO, a careful scrutiny was made of published materials, including environmental assessments of the Texaco project, and in-depth interviews were conducted with ten experts representing academia, government, the larger commercial fishery, the independent fishery, the media, the oil industry and the environmental lobby.

From this study, it was concluded that LASMO's project need not suffer the same fate as Texaco's if LASMO could prove that the project would not harm the environment and if LASMO could meet and successfully negotiate with the fishing community to prevent organized fishery opposition to the project.

Planning

It was clear that a careful strategy was necessary to obviate the potential for considerable opposition. The target audiences were identified as the independent and commercial fisheries, the federal, provincial and local governments, potential allies such as the Offshore Trade Association and the news media.

Four key messages were developed for these target audiences:

1. Oil from Cohasset and Panuke is extremely light, having the colour and consistency of a cup of weak tea.
2. The proposed production area is not heavily fished, is ice free and the seas are relatively calm.

3. LASMO's project is quite small, costing less than five per cent of the estimated cost for the Hibernia development planned for the North Atlantic off Newfoundland.
4. The production technology to be used for the project has been used successfully all over the world, so no new technological innovations are required.

LASMO were advised to avoid a general public announcement and the filing of applications which would automatically initiate public hearings, until productive discussions had been concluded with the identified opinion leaders. LASMO were advised to respond to media enquiries, emphasizing the four key messages, but to seek no publicity; in discussions with journalists, LASMO were advised to avoid discussion of the project schedule, indicating that the schedule would be dictated by the review process.

Implementation
In lieu of public meetings, the most senior LASMO executives met privately with fishery and environmental groups and with government officials, at both political and bureaucratic levels. During these meetings, LASMO executives listened first and then communicated the key messages. LASMO's credibility was enhanced by its early agreement to a comprehensive compensation plan for fishermen, in which any claims would be assessed by an independent group representing both the petroleum and the fishing industries.

An information pack, highlighting the key messages, was prepared for use as required, but no broadly based circulation was sought.

Media training was provided for LASMO executives and they were advised to seek one-to-one interviews, rather than news conferences.

Evaluation
The Canada-Nova Scotia Offshore Petroleum Board, in September 1990, approved LASMO's application to produce oil at Cohasset and Panuke. This will be Canada's first commercial offshore oil production.

There was no organized opposition to the project during the 18 months of LASMO's operations. The approval date of September 1990 was consistent with LASMO's internal project schedule.

An editorial in the region's leading daily newspaper, the *Chronicle-Herald*, commented:

LASMO took the lessons of Texaco's experience to heart . . . If LASMO had not taken so much pains to address the concerns of fishermen, it would not now be well on its way towards producing oil in Canada's first commercial offshore project.

The first oil came ashore on 5 June 1992 and was welcomed by the community. A reception was held to mark the occasion and a commemorative plaque was unveiled. Comment in the press was very supportive and the event was hailed as a wonderful development in the economic development of Nova Scotia. Typical newspaper headlines were: 'Offshore oil project fascinating and welcome'; 'Let it flow'; 'After 30 years it's offshore oil'.

Comment

This programme, which is summarized here, received the overall award of excellence in the 1991 International Public Relations Association Golden World Awards for Excellence. It is a very good example of how the quiet and gentle approach will often be more successful than a major frontal attack.

3

Comparison between public relations, propaganda, advertising and marketing

Public relations, propaganda, advertising and marketing all share somewhat similar objectives: to change attitudes, to influence public or private opinion or to encourage the purchase of goods or services. However, the methods employed to seek results are very different. While these four activities have certain factors in common, their ideology is quite different and while a combination of some of these may be employed at times, they are separate entities and should not be confused.

Lucien Matrat, a pioneer of public relations in France, has suggested how public relations can be differentiated from advertising and propaganda. He stated that, in his opinion, while they may all use the same tools and use similar forms of communication, their aims are not the same:

- Advertising seeks to boost the sale of goods or services — it is the strategy of desire.
- Propaganda is the strategy of conditioning. The aim of propaganda is to create a collective force and its assertions generally have no basis in verifiable fact.
- Public relations strategy, however, is based on trust and mutual understanding.

This evaluation of the essential differences between these three forms of communication was written by Lucien Matrat as long ago as 1971 but is just as valid today as when it was first propounded.

Public relations or propaganda?

For years, writers have endeavoured to analyze and explain the phenomenon of propaganda. The modern consensus is to judge it by reference to its aims. Some commentators might suggest that propaganda for evangelism is good, while propaganda for fascism is bad. Of course, in considering this question value judgments come into play immediately.

In 1988, the International Public Relations Association published *Gold Paper No 6 — Public Relations and Propaganda, values compared*. This monograph, by Professor Tim Traverse-Healy, outlines the historical background of the two concepts and describes the differences and similarities.

Put simply, the aim of propaganda is to build a movement or a following and there are varying degrees of source identification. Public relations, on the other hand, aims to achieve mutual understanding and consent through dialogue and there is always clear identification of the source of the message or activity. Public relations practitioners are required by their code of professional conduct to declare always on whose behalf they are working or issuing statements.

Another distinction which helps to differentiate these two activities is that propaganda is essentially a command mode, one sided, whereas the aim of public relations is to establish a dialogue and to achieve harmony and consent through two-way information, argument and discussion.

Public relations and other disciplines

It has been the practice of business schools and management colleges to place public relations, if they recognize it at all, within the syllabus of either marketing or advertising. A typical example is the MBA programme of the City University Business School in London where marketing is a core subject and the principles of advertising is one of the electives. This elective has ten sub-sections of which the Role of Public Relations is only one. Contrast this with the view of Sir John Harvey-Jones, and numerous CEOs in Britain and the USA, that the main concern of a company chairman should be strategic planning and public relations. Are not the MBAs of today destined to be the company chairmen of tomorrow?

If public relations is a part of marketing, one might expect that a comprehensive textbook on marketing would devote some pages to a summary of public relations. *Marketing Today* by Gordon Glover, (Prentice Hall, Third Edition) offers 'a broad, contemporary approach to the concepts and techniques of the marketing process'. Neither in the index nor in the text is there any mention of public relations.

It is comparatively easy to distinguish between advertising and public relations. Figure 3.1 contrasts the main characteristics of advertising with those of public relations practice.

The most significant difference is that in advertising one buys a space within which there is complete control of the text and presentation of the message, subject to certain legal and moral restraints. The timing of the appearance of the advertisement and the number of repeats is also completely under control. The effect, however, may be short-lived or nil, should that particular issue of the newspaper or magazine be not opened by members of the target audience.

Characteristic	Advertising	Public relations
Use of media	buys time or space	relies on gaining media coverage
Control of message	tight control of content and timing	relatively little control
Credibility of message	relatively low credibility	relatively high acceptance of message
Type of target audience	narrow target audiences, market related	specific publics or audiences
Focus of activity	market or sales oriented	attitude or situation oriented
Time scale	relatively short-term objectives	both short- and long-term objectives
Evaluation	established measurement techniques	relatively limited evaluation methods
Payment for agency	agencies paid mainly by commission from media	agencies paid by service fees based on time and/or annual retainer

Figure 3.1 *Characteristics of advertising compared with public relations practice*

Advertising and public relations are not mutually exclusive. Logically, advertising is part of public relations since its objective is to strengthen belief and to encourage change, albeit in purchasing habits rather than in general opinions. In some companies, the public relations department includes advertising and this arrangement can be very successful. It is more usual in large organizations for the two functions to be managed separately. In all cases, however, it is desirable to coordinate the general policy of both in line with the company's culture.

There are a number of instances where a public relations programme may include a substantial amount of advertising. The major example of this is the use by some large organizations of institutional advertising campaigns. The oil companies, for instance, use this method of trying to persuade motorists to use their particular brand of petrol because of the company's contribution to environmental protection, scientific research, corporate social responsibility or education.

Another important use of advertising in public relations is when it becomes necessary to reach an audience very quickly. An example is when a product recall becomes necessary. In financial public relations, a number of crisis situations may arise where immediate contact with shareholders becomes imperative. If there are a very large number of individuals on the share register, the most effective way of contacting them quickly is by advertising in the *Financial Times* and other quality newspapers.

Marketing and public relations

Mention has been made earlier in this chapter of the tendency to subsume the public relations function within marketing. Apart from an apparent desire by some managers for empire building, there is little justification for this attitude.

A comparison between the official definitions should clarify the confusion. The Chartered Institute of Marketing defines their field thus:

> Marketing is the management process responsible for identifying, anticipating and satisfying customers' requirements profitably.

The Institute of Public Relations defines public relations practice as:

> the planned and sustained effort to establish and maintain goodwill and understanding between an organization and its publics.

A comparison of these two definitions should make it clear that while they obviously share certain characteristics, the field of public relations practice is much wider than that of marketing. The proponents of marketing claim a very wide remit but have not yet claimed to cover parliamentary liaison, internal employee relations, community relations, crisis management, corporate social responsibility, environmental scanning and general involvement in corporate strategy and planning. All these activities are likely to come within the ambit of public relations if it is allowed to make its maximum contribution to success and efficiency.

Marketing writers emphasize that marketing is an exchange process which underlies the relationships between organizations and their customer/client groups. The exchange process usually involves four stages:

1. Seeking the understanding of the other party to the exchange.
2. Creating value, as perceived by the other party.
3. Sharing ideas about the value of products or services so that both parties share a common perception of value.

4. Delivering the goods or services through an actual, physical transaction between the parties.

It is obvious that public relations ideas and skills will play a valuable part in these processes, particularly in stages 2 and 3. It is seldom that any marketing programme will not include supporting public relations activities. The interrelationship is so close that there is no point in trying to separate these aspects of the typical marketing mix. Hence it is obvious that marketing executives need to understand public relations and public relations practitioners must appreciate the ways in which public relations can feature in marketing programmes.

Public relations working in support of marketing is often called business-to-business public relations and some practitioners concentrate on this aspect of their work. These activities are likely to include trade and consumer media relations, product launches, producing sales literature, organising trade shows and exhibition stands, and arranging sponsorships.

One might imagine that the concept of marketing would be fairly simple and that the difficulties would arise when planning and implementing a marketing campaign. However, some marketing gurus talk about widening the concept and suggest that marketing can be viewed as:

■ a set of organizational activities between a company and its customers;
■ an orientation requiring a company to be completely customer focused;
■ a social philosophy.

Summary

Marketing, advertising and public relations have many common interfaces but that is no excuse for trying to poach each other's territory. A large organization will almost certainly have both a marketing and public relations division. Their functions will sometimes come together and at other times be quite separate. Vauxhall Motors have solved this territory problem quite neatly. Public relations looks after name and reputation; marketing protects the brands.

4
Communicating with publics and specialized audiences

At the appropriate stage in public relations planning, the agreed programme will be implemented by communication. It then becomes essential to decide what should be communicated, to whom and by what methods.

Joseph Pulitzer, the American newspaper pioneer, stated his view of how to communicate which is still valid today.

> Put it before them
> *briefly* so they will read it
> *clearly* so they will appreciate it
> *picturesquely* so they will remember it, and above all
> *accurately* so they will be guided by its light.

These four principles can be a useful guide to our communicating philosophy, but need to be translated into positive plans of action.

We usually have two different reasons for communicating — for information or for persuasion. These two reasons are not mutually exclusive and it may be hoped that often sufficient accurate information will fulfil the persuasive requirement. It is difficult, however, and may be impossible to change public attitudes and opinions by communication alone, however convincing.

Communication requires a sender, a message, a medium and a receiver. It is the latter that presents the most difficulty since the message and the medium are under our direct control.

In this chapter we are concentrating on the receivers of the public relations messages. Terms which are sometimes used in public relations to denote the individuals or groups we wish to contact and influence at any particular time are audiences, constituencies or interest groups. However, we usually use the term 'publics' to avoid confusion. The use of the term audiences is not favoured as it seems to imply a passive reaction rather than the active or positive response we hope to achieve.

Identifying 'publics'

An organisation may have a vast range of individuals and groups with which it may wish to communicate. It is necessary to determine which are the most relevant publics at any particular time.

The publics of interest will usually be both internal and external. The internal publics of a large company will include full and part-time employees, management, trainees, trades union officials and managements and employees of subsidiary companies at home or overseas.

The external publics are likely to be more varied and the long list will include customers, suppliers and distributors; central and local government; financial interests; environmental and other pressure groups; the media, trade and professional associations; academic and research institutes and the general public.

The range of potential publics of an organization

Figure 4.1 shows diagrammatically the extremely wide range of publics that may be of concern to a typical company or organization. While it is desirable to keep in touch as much as possible with all these constituencies, it is impossible to target all these groups simultaneously.

In corporate communication, it is useful to consider four stages of sending out messages:

1st stage	—	seeking awareness (here is who we are);
2nd stage	—	involvement (here is what we can do for you);
3rd stage	—	communication (here is what we think);
4th stage	—	ethical persuasion (this is what we want you to believe or do).

It is obvious that the first two stages must be carried out effectively before there is much hope of success in the final two stages.

To achieve a logical plan for successful communication requires the synthesis of many different factors. This is shown in Figure 4.2 and the arrows indicate where feedback will influence the development of the integrated communication strategy and programme.

Progressing from Figure 4.2 which is a conceptual model of all the various factors involved, it is necessary to translate this into an **action plan**. Figure 4.3 is based on the manner in which a new subject — the environment and greening — was developed from an idea to an active nationwide campaign. In this figure, also, the arrows stress the importance of feedback and the interdependence of the different stages of the programme. There is ample evidence that this programme worked. Some years ago, only nature freaks were really concerned with ecology and the environment: today it is a matter of concern at both national and international levels.

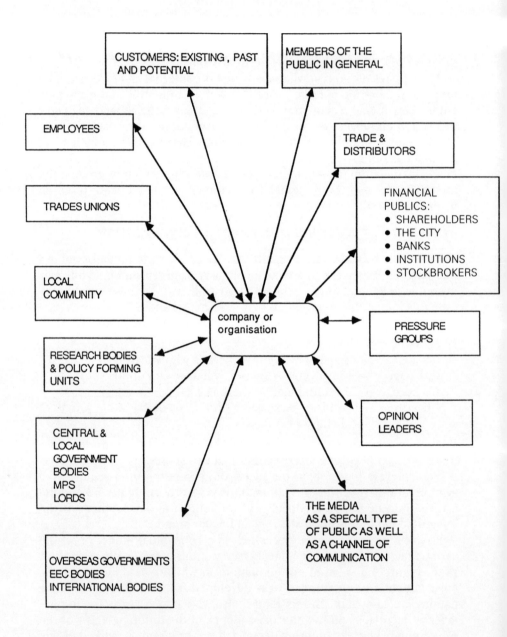

Figure 4.1 *The range of potential publics of an organization*

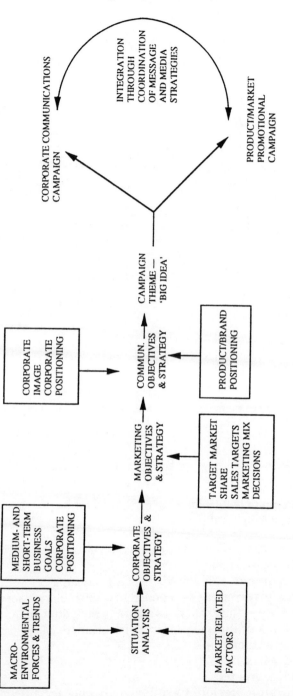

Figure 4.2 *Steps in the development of an integrated communications campaign*

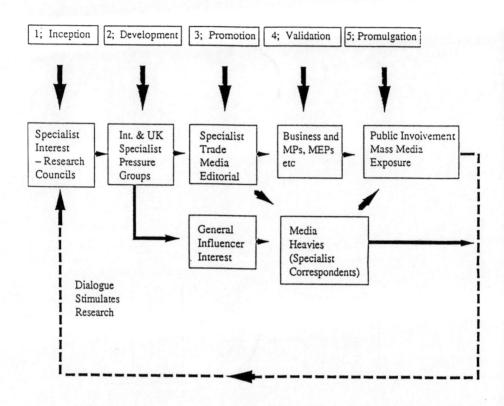

Figure 4.3 *Stages in the development and promulgation of a new idea*

One large manufacturing company has listed its publics of concern and key opinion formers thus:

- **The media** — *Print*: national, regional and local. *Electronic*: radio, tv, cable and satellite.
- **Government** — MPs, MEPs, civil servants.
- **Local government** — councillors, town clerks, senior executives.
- **The City** — investment community including analysts.
- **Captains of industry** — industrial leaders, suppliers, competitors.
- **Trade associations**.
- **Academics**.
- **Trades Unions**.
- **Environmental lobby groups** — Greenpeace, Friends of the Earth, other protest groups.

- **Local community.**
- **Employees.**

A public may be a small group or a vast group, but each with common interests or problems. Furthermore, any one person may belong to a number of different groups. For example, a worker in a factory may be also a consumer, a motorist, a parent, a householder, a voter, a local councillor and a DIY enthusiast.

In practice, we are more often concerned with specific publics rather than with the general public.

Public opinion

As much of our efforts are directed towards influencing public opinion it is necessary to consider the meaning of the term. *Webster's International Dictionary* gives three alternative meanings for public opinion.

1. The predominant attitude of a community.
2. The collective will of the people.
3. A summation of public expression regarding a specific issue.

Edward Bernays has stated the following:

- Public opinion is a term describing an ill-defined, mercurial and changeable group of individual judgments.
- It is the aggregate result of individual opinion — now uniform, now conflicting — of the men and women who make up society or any group of society.
- A person usually has settled opinions on most aspects of personal and public life. To change these opinions is difficult, sometimes impossible.

This quotation is from the first public relations textbook *Crystallizing public opinion* by Dr Edward L Bernays (published in 1923 in New York). It reveals a very shrewd judgment which has enabled Bernays to counsel top personalities in American political and business life for over 70 years. Now, at the age of 101, he is still lecturing and writing.

Influencing public opinion

Dr Bernays developed his ideas about public opinion in a further book *The Engineering of Consent* (published in 1955 by the University of Oklahoma). This book aroused some controversy as critics suggested that 'engineering' implied unethical action. A quotation from the book (Figure 4.4) shows that he was using the word engineering in the scientific sense which implies a plan. There is nothing sinister or underhand about persuasion, provided it is based on full information and truth and emanates from an overt source.

To be successful, or to stand a chance of success, persuasive communication requires the following:

- prior analysis of the identity and motivation of the sender;
- research into the existing relationship between sender and receiver;
- ability to identify priority receivers;
- knowledge of the composition and needs of the targeted audience;
- knowledge of communication processes and how attitudes can be modified;
- creation of messages in a form with audience appeal;
- identification of suitable channels of communication.

Bernays' viewpoint, as expressed in this book, can be summed up as positive action:

- to reinforce favourable opinions;
- to transform latent attitudes into positive beliefs;
- to modify or neutralize hostile or critical opinions.

Books on public relations usually place undue emphasis on the minutiae of public relations. They discuss the proper fashioning of the tools - selection of lists, rules for copy preparation, and other subjects - but neglect the guiding philosophy, the basic techniques which enable the tools to be used efficiently. It is as if books on surgery concerned themselves mainly with the shape and sharpness of surgical instruments and how to wield them.

Public relations is the attempt, by information, persuasion, and adjustment, to engineer public support for an activity, cause, movement or institution. Professionally, its activities are planned and executed by trained practitioners in accordance with scientific principles, based on the findings of social scientists.

Evidences of the power of public opinion prove to every man the necessity of understanding the public, of adjusting to it, of informing it, or winning it over. The ability to do so is the test of leadership.

It is necessary not only for professionals to understand public relations, but also for laymen, who must look to experts for advice. Executives who use professional advice need to know how to appraise the expert . . . . . In public relations, the client or employer who cannot appraise the expert is seriously handicapped. Public relations can be correctly evaluated only through a clear understanding of the public relations process.

Extracts from Ed Bernays' introductory chapter in 'The engineering of consent' ed. Bernays, University of Oklahoma Press, 1955

Figure 4.4 *Extracts from Ed Bernays' introductory chapter in 'The engineering of consent'*

Hadley Cantril's laws of public opinion

In his book *Gauging Public Opinion* (Princeton University Press, 1944) Hadley Cantril propounded some very pertinent comments on public opinion as the following extracts show:

1. Opinion is highly sensitive to important events.
2. Events of unusual magnitude are likely to swing public opinion temporarily from one extreme to another.
3. Opinion is determined more by events than by words.
4. Verbal statements are more effective when listeners have to seek some interpretation from a reliable source.
5. By and large, public opinion does not anticipate emergencies — it only reacts to them.
6. Opinion is basically based on self-interest.
7. Once self-esteem is involved, opinion is not easily changed.
8. People are less reluctant to have critical decisions made by their leaders if they feel that somehow they were taking some part in the decision.
9. Public opinion, like personal opinion, is coloured by desire.
10. The important psychological dimensions of opinion are direction, intensity, breadth and depth.

Selecting the audiences

It is quite impossible to reach all potential publics simultaneously, so the selection of priority targets is a prerequisite for formulating an effective communication plan. Figure 4.5 shows graphically one method of planning audience selection. It stresses the need to define audiences, assign priorities and attempt to identify gatekeepers.

Influence of opinion formers

Most people are greatly influenced by the opinions of others, particularly of those they respect. These individuals are usually referred to as 'opinion leaders'. They can be classified in two categories:

1. Those who are formal leaders by virtue of rank or position. They can be members of Parliament, editors, teachers or clergy.
2. Informal opinion leaders who by virtue of charisma, personality or background exert a strong influence on their peers, friends or acquaintances.

It is obvious that in striving to modify attitudes or beliefs it is time effective to concentrate on trying to influence opinion leaders who, in

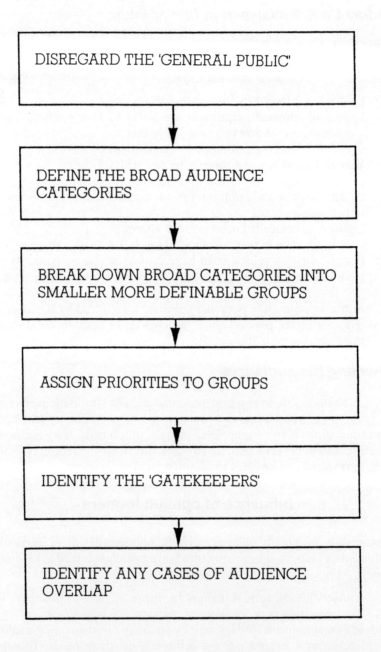

Figure 4.5 *The stages in defining target audiences for a public relations programme*

turn, are likely to spread understanding to ever-widening circles. This phenomenon is usually described as the **multiplying factor**, whereby any change of attitude or belief of the opinion leader is maximized by reflection to other sections of the public. It has been estimated that 90 per cent of views are influenced strongly by the 10 per cent who are opinion leaders.

The availability of computers has made it possible to envisage the ideal solution to this question of communicating directly with specific publics. A company can begin to prepare its own database of organizations and individuals of current or likely potential interest. If this database is built up carefully and kept up to date it can provide at any time an accurate list of the specific publics likely to be interested in any particular issue. The ability to have available such an accurate and customized mailing list would obviate the necessity to disseminate information widely in the hope that some of the messages would reach the desired targets.

Unquestioning reliance on targeting opinion leaders has been queried by some researchers. More studies on this subject are desirable, either to confirm conventional belief or to suggest better ways of targeting communication for public relations purposes.

Doubt has been expressed about the wisdom of basing a whole programme on reaching priority groups or individuals with the message and ignoring less important ones. How are the opinion leaders expected to perform and exercise their power? Is their function merely to act as gatekeepers who give the communicator access to important persons or are they expected to embellish, translate or simplify the communicators' messages? Or is the opinion leader's role primarily to act as an authority whose endorsement attests to the legitimacy of a message?

A broader theoretical question asks if these opinion leaders can absorb all the messages which may be directed at them. What is likely to happen if hundreds of professional communicators compete for the limited time, attention and effect of these relatively few people? Do they learn to set up effective defences against all kinds of information programmes or do they have the time and energy to distinguish between (for them) trivial or significant causes? Perhaps they learn to ignore all efforts to reach them with special pleading. It would be ironic if the efforts by communicators to reach these high priority audiences were to result in their becoming immunized to these messages.

Communication audits

This term is often used to denote intelligence gathering for public relations purposes. An audit suggests a very careful and detailed study but the majority one comes across are often very short on data and very long on opinion.

A communication audit can be used to measure the effectiveness of existing internal and external communication systems and to identify the factors affecting their operation. It will thus provide a sound basis for formulating new public relations policies.

The public relations department of a large company should be competent itself to carry out the communication audit of the organization but it is possible to call on the services of consultants who specialize in this field. This is similar to the way in which management consultants are often called in, at considerable expense, to tell the Board what it could have found out for itself.

A typical communication audit might make the following points in its final report:

1. The company appears to do an excellent job in protecting the environment.
2. It is aware of its social responsibilities.
3. It cares about the health and safety of employees.
4. It communicates regularly with employees through publications and regular meetings.
5. It has an excellent employee benefits programme.
6. It is positive in its advertising and marketing programmes.
7. It keeps all its external publics well informed about company activities and future plans.

Such a remarkably good audit report would be well received by management, but an unfavourable one should receive an equally good reception as it would point to weaknesses requiring urgent attention.

A favourable audit should be repeated in perhaps three years, an unfavourable one needs repetition as soon as steps have been taken to remedy the identified shortcomings.

How effective is your communication?

Effective communication — effective in the sense that it will be understood and acted upon — is very difficult to achieve. Professor Osmo A Wiio, of the University of Helsinki, has amused himself by acting as devil's advocate in formulating the following alternative laws of communication which challenge existing assumptions.

Wiio's laws of communication:

1. Communication usually fails — except by chance. Human communication is often as low as five per cent. Success of that magnitude approaches statistical randomness.
    1.1 If communication can fail — it will.
    1.2 If communication cannot fail — it nevertheless, usually fails.

1.3 If communication seems to succeed in the way which was intended, it must be in a way which was not intended. If everything seems to go fine, the success may be illusory. The receiver may think he understands your message but in reality he misunderstands it — or understands it in his own way.

1.4 If you are satisfied that your communication is bound to succeed then your communication is bound to fail. To be content with communication usually means that you designed the communication process for yourself and not for the receiver. The first rule of effective communication is to think about the receiver and create messages for him

2. If a message can be understood in different ways it will be understood in the way which does the most harm.

3. There is always somebody who knows better than you what you meant with your message.

4. The more communication there is the more difficult it is for communication to succeed.

4.1 The more communication there is the more misunderstandings will occur. There is a naive belief that increased communication is always for the better — but experience suggests otherwise.

5. In mass communication it is not important how things *are*, the important thing is how things *seem to be*. Mass media sccm to create their own reality which often has very little to do with 'observable reality'.

6. The importance of a news item is inversely proportional to the square of the distance.

Professor Wiio explains that his cynicism springs from attending too many meetings and hearing so many unproven and often totally wrong expectations about the effect of human communication.

The lesson for public relations practitioners to learn from these critical comments is the need to increase efforts to understand the way in which recipients of messages are likely to react.

Financial public relations and investor relations

While the practice of public relations is based on the same principles whatever field is being considered, the financial world introduces a number of special rules and constraints which makes this area a veritable minefield for those without specialized knowledge of the City, the Stock Exchange and the special circumstances which surround financial matters and investor relations.

All public companies which are quoted on the Stock Exchange are subject to the perceptions of the market. Every large company has to consider the effect of its policies on a number of different constituencies. These include:

- investors, shareholders and 'the City';
- customers and suppliers;
- central and local government;
- the financial press and other media;
- trade associations and trade unions;
- local communities and educational bodies.

All the usual considerations about public relations which have been described in earlier chapters apply also to the financial world but there are extra requirements which necessitate special attention.

An example of the special care required in takeover situations was highlighted by the report of the Panel on Takeovers and Mergers which criticized a merchant bank and a leading public relations consultancy over apparent leaks in the market during the bid defence conducted on behalf of Dowly International. This report is important because the Panel stated clearly that merchant bankers are responsible for controlling all information released during such circumstances.

Target audiences

Dealing with audiences in financial public relations is often called investor relations or IR, but there does not appear to be any justification for sub-dividing the field since IR is certainly a part of financial relations. This concept leads to a call for a large company to have an investor relations director in addition to the finance director. It is, of course, the prerogative of any organization to arrange its board responsibilities in the manner it chooses, but the modern tendency to confer new titles for existing tasks tends to be confusing and non-productive. Comment has been made earlier on the growing tendency to use titles such as public affairs, corporate relations or head of communications to denote public relations. The use of investor relations instead of the well-established title financial public relations is a further example of unnecessary obfuscation.

The target audiences can be summed up as: institutional and private investors; brokers and analysts and the financial press. Each of these groups will require differing approaches. In the UK, a smaller proportion of shares are held by private investors and the power of the fund managers is very strong. The chairman of The Boots Company plc, Robert Gunn, has stated that while they concentrate on their relations with the major institutions who are the key decision makers, they do not forget the importance of communicating with small investors. Relationships between companies and their institutional shareholders have been changing due to the liberalization of financial markets, the continuing restructuring of British industry into larger units and the growing internationalization of trade within the European Community and other trading blocs.

In March 1989, the Confederation of British Industry (CBI) published a very good guide to financial matters: *Improving Investor Relations — a Business Guide.* This is a detailed explanation of the factors which require careful attention. This book was published primarily for the information of managers but many of the factors discussed come within the field of financial public relations.

Working in investor relations calls for professionalism, honesty, tact and sensitivity. The requirements of the regulatory bodies have to be adhered to strictly and the Investor Relations Society provides a forum for the discussion of best practice.

The main function of financial public relations is to:

- promote the company's credibility and reputation;
- establish good communication links with the financial press and the media;
- identify and broaden the company's shareholder base;
- defend against takeovers;
- assist in the identification of acquisitions;
- improve internal communication and employee motivation.

Methods used in financial public relations

The case history of how Trusthouse Forte convinced City audiences of the correctness of their decision to change the company name to Forte, described in Chapter 2, illustrates the many different actions necessary to secure an orderly transformation of this kind. The different stages were:

- research to establish a base for a strategic plan;
- deciding the key messages which would be used for communication;
- designing and preparation of the corporate materials which would be used to explain the proposed changes;
- informing shareholders through the annual report;
- direct approach to analysts and institutional investors.

Consumerism

The initial defensive attitude towards consumerism on the part of manufacturers has, over some forty years, changed to a realization that a positive approach to consumer likes and dislikes can help the orderly development of design, manufacture and marketing.

Most manufacturers now welcome their contacts with the official consumer organizations and benefit from these contacts in a number of ways:

- Accurate information on the preferences of consumers is a valuable guide to the introduction of new products and helps to ensure that they will not be surprised by changes in public tastes.
- Providing accurate information to consumers establishes a bond of sympathy which helps to cement customer loyalty.
- Feedback from customers provides valuable data on quality and performance.

A consumer relations code

In the US they like to categorize relationships and the US Chamber of Commerce has published a useful set of guidelines in a 10 point consumer relations code:

1. Protect the health and safety of consumers in the design and manufacture of products and the provision of services.
2. Utilize advancing technology to produce goods that meet the highest standards of quality at the lowest reasonable price.
3. Seek out the informed views of consumers and other groups to help assure consumer satisfaction.
4. Simplify, clarify and honour warranties and guarantees.
5. Maximize the quality of product servicing and repairs and encourage their fair pricing.
6. Eliminate frauds and deceptions from the market place.
7. Ensure that sales personnel know their products.
8. Provide consumers with objective information.
9. Facilitate sound value comparisons.
10. Provide effective channels for receiving and acting on consumer complaints and suggestions.

The last point in this code deserves careful attention. Letters of complaint from customers should always be dealt with expeditiously and fully. They should not be regarded as a nuisance as they can yield useful information on the quality and performance of products under actual working conditions (too many 'bug letters' are still being sent out by companies who should know better).

Case history 6
A proactive approach by Whirlpool

The US Whirlpool Corporation, a major appliance manufacturer, has adopted a positive approach to relations with consumers since 1964.

The Whirlpool programme, which has six main features, was designed to attack the main sources of annoyance among appliance buyers. These included obscure warranties, service problems, lack of knowledge about correct operation and frustrating inability to get somebody interested in their difficulties.

The six features of the Whirlpool programme are:

1. A 'cool line' that permits appliance owners to make free telephone calls to the company headquarters in Benton Harbour, Michigan when they have any questions about the operation of their equipment. Trained engineers at the Michigan HQ answer these calls. In the first three years of this service, they received 40 000 calls for help.
2. The company honours all warranties itself and does not depend on local distributors.
3. Warranties are written in clear, simple language.
4. Publicity and sales material give maximum information to help customers make wise buying decisions.
5. National advertising, 20 per cent of the total advertising budget, tells customers about the 'cool line', and encourages them to telephone headquarters whenever they need help, advice or reassurance.
6. An effective programme of internal education impresses upon all Whirlpool employees and staff the critical importance of assuring customer satisfaction and confidence.

Comment
This excellent example of a comprehensive consumer public relations programme, designed to achieve maximum customer satisfaction, is worthy of emulation by other manufacturers.

Case history 7
Seeking direct contact with consumers

General Foods Corporation, one of the largest US manufacturers and distributors of packaged foods, has for a number of years conducted various programmes to ascertain consumer likes and dislikes and to impart information to consumers.

The company bases these efforts on its conviction that consumer confidence in its products, the essential ingredient for its continued growth, is founded not only on satisfaction in use, but on adequate consumer information and evidence of the company's concern for its customers' best interests.

Comment
This is obviously an expensive and time consuming policy, but General Foods obviously considers it cost-effective and an indispensable element in

winning and maintaining their share of the market.

The health care field

The role of public relations in the health care field has been developed for many years in the United States but is of more recent origin in Britain. It covers two main areas — giving information and advice about health, disease and mortality; and efforts to make the provision of medical care and treatment more readily available and user friendly.

For years, every hospital in the US had its own public relations department but this is a comparatively new idea in Britain. The growth of self-governing hospital trusts is likely to accelerate the introduction of public relations into the hospital scene. A successful hospital needs cooperation between its main constituents — the consultant, medical and nursing staffs, the administrators and the patients who come for diagnosis and treatment. Good internal communication is just as important here as in any industrial establishment. Harmony and cooperation require planned programmes to promote understanding and efficiency.

The public interest in everything to do with health, disease and the National Health Service continues to grow in geometrical progression. The pharmaceutical industry has its critics but its industrial base increases steadily. In the United Kingdom, it is expected that the 'over the counter' (OTC) sales of drugs will expand dramatically as the Government seeks to keep the soaring costs of the NHS under control. These circumstances will greatly increase the opportunities for public relations in the health care field. This area shares with the financial sector the weight of rules and regulations governing communication direct to the public. There are different rules for ethicals (medicines only available through prescription) and OTC products. Ethicals are covered by the code of practice of the Proprietary Association of Great Britain.

The methods of communication are similar to those used in other fields — media relations, education campaigns, advertising and sales materials, but the role of third party endorsement is very important. It is noteworthy that an increasing number of case studies in this area are being submitted in competition and winning awards. In the 1991 IPRA Golden World Awards for Excellence, trophies and certificates were won by the following:

- Wellcome Foundation for 'Cold sores, don't suffer in silence'.
- African Primary Health Care Promotion.
- Prostate cancer awareness week in the US.
- Rural health care in the Philippines.

- The promotion of organ donation in Israel.
- For a world without leprosy — campaign in Turkey.
- Aids intervention project in Kenya.
- Breast health campaign in Australia.
- European donor hospital education programme in Holland.

This list of case studies, entered in one competition in a single year, gives an indication of the positive contribution that public relations can make to different aspects of health.

Case history 8
The story of Bathsheba and King David

This well known biblical story was depicted by Rembrandt in 1654, with his common law wife, Hendrickje Stoffels as the model. To an art lover, this is a classic Rembrandt painting, but to a doctor it is a classic example of an early breast cancer.

This fact was used to great effect by an Australian public relations consultant, Kathie Melocco, on behalf of the Medical Benefits Fund of Australia, in a campaign to encourage women in Sydney to seek early detection of breast cancer at the MBF Sydney Square Breast Clinic. The painting shows Bathsheba holding a letter from King David asking her to meet him in secret, a meeting which was to have tragic consequences. The painting of the left breast of the model in the painting shows the distinctive dimpling which is now recognized as an early sign of breast cancer.

The campaign was very successful and enquiries at the clinic increased by 700 per cent. A similar campaign was introduced in other Australian east coast cities.

Comment
This is a striking example of the successful use of a 'gimmick' which had a direct relationship to the purpose of the campaign. Its novelty, coupled with its empathy and vital information had a wide appeal and assured the success of this important health conservation programme.

5

Media relations and parliamentary liaison

Public relations developed in the United States of America out of press agentry in the early days of the twentieth century, and for many years press relations was the major part of public relations as it was practised in both the USA and Europe. Pioneers such as Edward Bernays called themselves consultants or counsellors but most practitioners provided a press service for their employers or clients.

By the time public relations became firmly established in Britain, from 1946 onwards, the Institute of Public Relations insisted on the comprehensive nature of public relations practice, but in those early days most practitioners offered only a press relations service.

In Chapter 1, the comprehensive parameters of public relations have been described, but nevertheless press relations have remained a very important part of most programmes. With the onset of radio and television, the term press relations has been replaced by the title **media relations** and press conferences are now described as **news conferences**.

A typical issue of a daily newspaper in Britain includes a very substantial amount of news and comments which have been supplied or suggested by public relations sources. These published items can have quite a powerful influence on public opinion, especially in the financial sector. If an organization is in the public domain and its activities are likely to be of public interest or curiosity, the press will publish reports and comments, and possibly photographs. This will happen whether or not they receive any cooperation from those concerned. If journalists *do* receive help, however, the items published are likely to be more accurate, less garbled and less likely to cause embarrassment. This relates to serious journalism and does not cover the antics of some tabloid papers when they scent a real or imaginary scandal.

Liaison with the media

Apart from supplying information, there are many opportunities for a company to initiate beneficial news items and features. It follows, therefore, that it is desirable to attempt to establish friendly relations with journalists and editors of relevant publications. Daily newspapers are more glamorous than trade and technical publications, although informed comment in the latter may have more beneficial results.

It is good policy to take the media representatives into your confidence whenever possible. Public relations should never be a barrier between the media and an organization; rather it should always aim to be a bridge across which news and information can travel both ways without hindrance. Some trade associations have regular meetings — perhaps over lunch — with editors of relevant trade journals at which information is given 'off the record'. At such meetings, the editors often impart more information than they receive. Similar meetings are often held with individual editors, but the synergetic effect of a few people meeting together and discussing topics of mutual interest can yield beneficial results.

A large company will usually have a press office, or a press officer, and it may be company policy for all media enquiries to be routed, in the first instance, via the press office. This arrangement is logical and works well provided it is an enabling procedure and not employed as a barrier between the media and senior management. This is where common sense should prevail. If a journalist gets through to a senior executive of the company, initial questions should be answered and then a suggestion made that fuller details would be available from the press officer. Complete refusal to say anything may suggest there is something to hide.

Media relations is, for many companies, the most important part of public relations, but it must always be integrated with and compatible with the overall public relations policy of the organization.

The fundamental requirement for working successfully with any branch of the media must be an understanding of how they operate and their requirements. It was often suggested in the past — and this belief may still persist — that a good public relations practitioner must have started as a journalist. This is not necessarily true since it is not difficult to acquire a comprehensive understanding of journalism and media production. In fact, the qualities of a good journalist are somewhat different from those required in public relations practice. Many of the leading public relations practitioners in Britain today started their careers in journalism, but many journalists have found working in public relations more demanding than they expected and have been glad to revert to their former occupation. This situation is likely to change as an increasing number of students in Britain graduate from undergraduate and postgraduate public relations degree programmes which have included journalistic and writing experience.

Methods of working with the media

The main requirement of working with the media is giving them what they need, in a convenient format and at the correct time. The usual methods are still through direct contact, by issuing news releases, holding news conferences, using press agencies, and possibly the new concept of video news releases (VNR).

Direct contact with a journalist is obviously the best way to achieve results but time constraints make this the exception rather than the rule. A danger to avoid is any misunderstanding about statements which may be 'off the record', or which are usable without direct attribution.

Media training builds confidence

Company senior executives are called upon increasingly to give interviews on radio or television. Media training is readily available in London and other main centres and a series of training sessions is a good idea for anybody likely to be involved with the media.

The dangers of 'no comment'

It requires some skill to be able to say 'no' without alienating the journalist who is asking the questions. Some people apparently think it is clever to respond with a firm 'no comment'. Such an abrupt response is rude, not clever and is hardly likely to help to establish good relations with the journalist or other members of the media. It may also suggest that you have some dark secrets to conceal.

A better solution is to tell the reporter exactly *why* it is not possible to answer the question and to discuss the subject in any detail: because negotiations have reached a delicate stage, or the wage discussions are still proceeding, or you have not yet received the full report, or relatives have not yet been informed. Any reply of this kind will give the reporter something that can be attributed but you have not divulged any sensitive information.

Accuracy is very important in answering media enquiries. They may well publish incorrect figures or wrong names but do not compound this possibility by failing to give out very accurate information at the outset.

Timing is very important because if the subject is topical the reporter will wish to meet the paper's deadline. Any promises to provide additional information or to supply photographs must be honoured and supplied at the agreed time.

Humour can be effective in dealing with criticism. Remember the apocryphal story that McDonalds were accused of using earthworms in their hamburgers. The company is supposed to have told the press that this story was untrue and that they would never use worms as they cost more per pound than good beef!

Some practitioners responsible for dealing with the media fail in their work because of the lack of advance planning. Care should be taken to anticipate awkward questions so that suitable answers can be given without delay which could allow rumours to circulate.

A press officer is unlikely to be technically qualified and if so should take the trouble to acquire the jargon and a basic knowledge sufficient to answer routine questions. If also helps if there is good relations with the technical experts in the company who can be contacted quickly.

News releases

Thousands of news releases are issued each year and many of them will be discarded by the recipients because of a number of elementary mistakes. It has been 'guesstimated' that more than 100 million news releases are sent out in the UK each year and that of these, only about three per cent are used. This certainly demonstrates that news releases must be well written and presented and contain news if they are likely to be successful.

A news release is a communication between two people and the normal rules about clear and easy communication apply. In more leisurely times, the news release was intended to interest the journalist in a subject worthy of investigation. The recipient might telephone to ask additional questions in order to compare the information received with comment received from other sources. Today, however, this treatment is only possible for major stories or incidents. Thus a news release has to stand on its own merits and is more likely to be used if it is supplied in a convenient form, without ambiguity and emanates from a source found in the past to be reliable.

The usual practice is to send out news releases to all the newspapers and other appropriate publications and not to send them out only to friends. However, in some instances a good alternative may be to send out the news to only two non-competitive publications on an exclusive basis.

If a news release is prepared for general issue, it is desirable to have at least two different versions. The version which is suitable for the quality newspapers is unlikely to be equally suitable for the technical and trade press which will require more detail, especially if the subject is a technical one. Ideally, a customized release would be prepared for each publication but this is seldom practicable and usual practice is to limit it to two or three versions.

The first paragraph of a release should give all the vital information: **what, where, why, who** and **when**. This gives the journalist enough information to decide if it is worth reading the whole release. Furthermore, if the news release is used to fill a small space so that only the first paragraph can be printed, the essential facts will have been included. It is usual for a release to be shortened, when necessary, by progressively cutting off the last paragraph. For this reason, it is wise to cover the full story in the first paragraph and then to develop the details progressively in subsequent paragraphs.

Rules for preparing a news release

Editors and journalists will welcome major news items sent to them in any format. The more run-of-the-mill news items are more likely to be welcomed and used if they are received in conventional style. The following are some of the more important rules to follow in preparing news releases:

1. Always use one side of the paper; the text should be double spaced and typewritten (or printed).
2. The identity of the sender must be stated clearly, and if the release is being issued by a consultancy on behalf of a client, the consultancy details must also be given. The release should always include contact names and telephone numbers for outside office hours.
3. A title should be given at the head of the release but this should be short and descriptive. There is no need to spend time trying to think up a clever headline as editors prefer to choose their own titles.
4. The wording of the release should be clear and unambiguous and hyperbole must be avoided. Do not underline any words and only use capitals for proper nouns or registered names.
5. It is desirable to keep the release to two A4 pages — or one A4 page if possible. If the subject is technical or complicated the details can be the subject of a separate document, rather than incorporated into one release.
6. Most of these rules are very practical and designed to help the recipient deal with it. For this reason, there should be wide margins and it is unwise to use up too much space with fancy headings.

Using photographs

Many news releases are reinforced by the addition of photographs. In suitable cases, it is a good plan to organize a photocall at which press photographers can take their own pictures. In other circumstances, it may be appropriate to make photographs available to the press. There are several different ways in which this can be effected. It is wasteful to include photographs in all press kits and it is better to indicate which photographs are available on request. All photographs must be captioned and the method of choice is to give the caption on a piece of paper which hangs down in front of the picture. Sticking the caption on the back of the photograph is not recommended as it makes it difficult in use.

Photography has many uses in public relations and this is discussed in Chapter 6.

The use and misuse of embargoes

Releases should normally be issued for immediate use and the heading should include the words 'immediate', or state a time and date. It is unwise to attempt to embargo the use of the release until some stipulated time ahead. Embargoes will usually only be respected by the media if the embargo is in their own interest. For example, the press welcome advance knowledge of complicated reports, or the Honours List, or other items which require careful study before publication, or are subject to Parliamentary privilege. In all other cases, the editor will ignore the embargo and may well discard the release in disgust at the amateurism of the sender.

Distribution of releases

It is important to see that the media receive your news quickly. You can do this yourself by mail or courier, or you can utilize the services of a specialist organization which provides a comprehensive production and delivery service. The growing availability of fax machines has helped to make communication easier and quicker but fax should not be used as a routine method of distribution.

A new development is the availability of video news releases (VNR). This is a sophisticated development of a service which has been available for many years for the distribution of cassette tapes to radio stations. VISNEWS is one of several companies which now offer this service. They issue, on behalf of subscribers, video news releases which are comprehensive press packs for television stations which broadcast standard film and relevant story angles to illustrate the story. The cost may be between £3000–5000 per item, depending on the item, but the results achieved have been quite impressive. The companies offering VNR services are set up to distribute material worldwide and to tailor the material for different markets, thus providing a really international service.

Public relations wire services have been available for many years and they customize the material sent in by subscribers before distributing the items nationally or worldwide.

The correct use of news conferences

An alternative to sending out information by issuing news releases is to invite the media to be represented at a news conference. This is a very useful device if used with discretion. If your organization gets the reputation of calling news conferences unnecessarily, the attendance will dwindle and possibly dry up completely.

There are three valid reasons for calling a news conference:

1. When the news item requires the showing of models or solid items.
2. If the subject of the conference is very important and likely to engender many questions.
3. If there is important background information to impart.

Invitations to news conferences are usually sent out about one week ahead. The invitation should give enough detail to encourage the editor's decision to send a representative, but not too much information to reveal the news in advance. Editors seldom reply to invitations so it is customary to check up by telephone a day or two before the event.

The venue should be selected to suit the press but it is convenient to hold it at your headquarters if they are easily accessible. If the venue is out of London, it is advisable to make arrangements to transport the party from London by air, rail or coach as appropriate. It is important to give clear, unambiguous instructions to those planning to attend. The initial invitation should state if the travel will be provided free of charge.

If the story is of general interest, it is impossible to select a time that will suit all the media. It is usual to call the conference for 11 or 11.30 am which suits the majority of those likely to attend.

Press kits should be prepared and handed out to participants after the speeches and questions. If journalists do not attend, they should be sent a press kit immediately after the event.

A news conference is an important event and careful planning is necessary both for the arrangements at the venue and the speech programme. The chair at the conference is normally taken by the senior member of the organization but if he or she is not a good speaker, another person should deliver the main speech and answer questions.

Question time is a very important part of any news conference and some organizers plant some questions in the audience to ensure that the question time will get off to a smooth start. This questionable practice is backed up by giving the speaker recommended answers to the planted questions. This can lead, as it has done on a number of occasions, to the speaker finishing the main speech and then continuing straight on with the answers to the questions before they have been asked. This causes unnecessary confusion. If the subject of the news conference is of interest to the journalists invited, there is seldom a dearth of questions.

It is helpful if a buffet lunch is provided as this provides an opportunity for journalists to mingle with the company executives present and to discuss matters which particularly interest them. It is essential that the initial invitation should state clearly what hospitality, if any, will be offered.

Some news conferences are attended, by invitation, by guests who are not media representatives. This is not a wise practice as journalists tend to resent the attendance of outsiders at serious conferences. Another kind of news conference which is held for social purposes is suitable for a mixed audience. Such an event, which does not have to be tied up necessarily with topical news, is usually held in the late afternoon and is a much more relaxed type of event.

Facility visits

Visits to factories or installations are an excellent way of imparting information as most people are more impressed by what they see than by what they are told. Facility visits are arranged for journalists, either in groups or individually. Similar visits are arranged for important customers and buyers or for the public, but preferably not at the same time as press visits.

The arrangements can be rather similar for each category but the actual programme of the visit must be planned carefully in view of the objective of the invitation. It is essential that the planning be carried out carefully and with imagination as a badly organized event will have the opposite result and will lose friends instead of gaining them.

'Letters to the editor'

The correspondence columns of the national, regional and local press offer a good opportunity to seek public notice for a point of view or to respond to criticism.

If a letter is written to correct a mistake or an ambiguity it is important not to repeat the error as this may bring the mistake or criticism to the notice of many who have missed the first publication. It is unethical to sign letters with fictitious names and, in general, if a letter is sent on behalf of an organization it should be signed by a senior executive rather than by a member of the public relations department.

Letters should be kept as short as possible as this will help to get them published. Moreover, if a letter is long it may be published in a shortened form which may distort its argument.

Radio and television

The future structure of radio and television in the UK may change considerably during the 1990s but there will always be opportunities for liaison with radio and tv producers who will continue to require material for news and feature programmes. Local radio stations are more likely to be receptive to news items and suggestions for programmes than national stations. Local stories, however, must be tailored to community interest.

The key to success in placing stories with radio or tv will depend on the effort made to understand the needs of these media and to establish good relations with them.

Measuring the results of media relations

The early attempts to measure the results of press relations relied on securing copies of stories printed and measuring the column inches. Press cutting bureaux can be used to supply cuttings and it is also possible to secure copies of items on radio and television. However, press cuttings are merely evidence that items have been printed but measurement alone can be misleading. If column inches are to mean anything, it is necessary to consider where the story appeared and in which edition and on which pages. In other words, to add a qualitative dimension to the plain measurement. The circulation of the publication and its readership profile must also be taken into account. Several companies now offer a scientific analysis of press cuttings but their accuracy remains to be established beyond doubt.

Too many media evaluation schemes measure output rather than impact. It is difficult to monitor press coverage accurately, but it is even more difficult to assess its impact in producing changes of attitude in target audiences or increase in sales.

To understand the value of public relations to a company, it is vital to understand how that company's image, products and activities are projected by the relevant media. However, collecting and reading press clippings is only half the answer. What does it all mean, and how does it affect a company's ability to take the right action?

One London company, Infopress Ltd, has developed a computerized scheme which claims to measure in detail the impact of media campaigns. The scheme, which is called IMPACT, has been developed to measure the effectiveness of media relations work in delivering messages to target audiences via print and broadcast media. Coverage (press cuttings, radio tapes etc) are collected continuously and transmitted to independent evaluators who mark them according to a prearranged schedule. The results give statistical indications of the impact of media campaigns and permit evaluation and forward planning of further media programmes.

CARMA International measures and evaluates media coverage to provide usable management intelligence. CARMA analyzes all forms of media to produce detailed statistical data, evaluates the results and provides concise but comprehensive reports on all relevant aspects. The client receives objective, easily assimilated information.

The criteria adopted vary from client to client so as to meet individual needs. CARMA identifies emerging issue and product trends, tracks competitors' strategies, legislative initiatives or the impact of specific activities and campaigns. Journalists are identified and favourability of coverage assessed. This information allows its users to tailor campaigns to very specific targets and allocate budgets with greater precision.

6
Methods of public relations

When a public relations programme has been agreed, after preliminary research and detailed discussion, the plan will usually include a number of different methods of communicating the message to priority publics and possibly also in some instances to the general public.

Media relations usually features prominently in most programmes and this has been discussed in the previous chapter. There are a number of other techniques which may be used – the printed word, the spoken word, exhibitions and conferences, lobbying and parliamentary relations and sponsorship. These methods of public relations have certain features in common but have varying objectives and employ an armoury of different methods so require individual consideration.

Three contrasting programmes

Public relations, as a management function, has an important part to play in the discussion and formulation of corporate strategy and other activities at that level, but it has many other duties to perform within a typical company or when working for an organization. Figure 6.1 illustrates the different levels of responsibility within a typical programme.

The following three examples contrast public relations programmes carried out for the Malaysian Government, the electronic giant Canon, and the Barbican Arts and Conference Centre in London.

'Visit Malaysia Year 1990'

This was the theme of a comprehensive programme launched by the Malaysian Government to increase the number of tourists. The programmes included the following:

- the production of promotional videos;
- media relations on an international scale;
- sponsorship deals with a number of major companies such as Coca-Cola;
- inviting travel journalists for fact-finding visits;

- production of many new items of promotional literature;
- exhibition stands at suitable travel and leisure exhibitions.

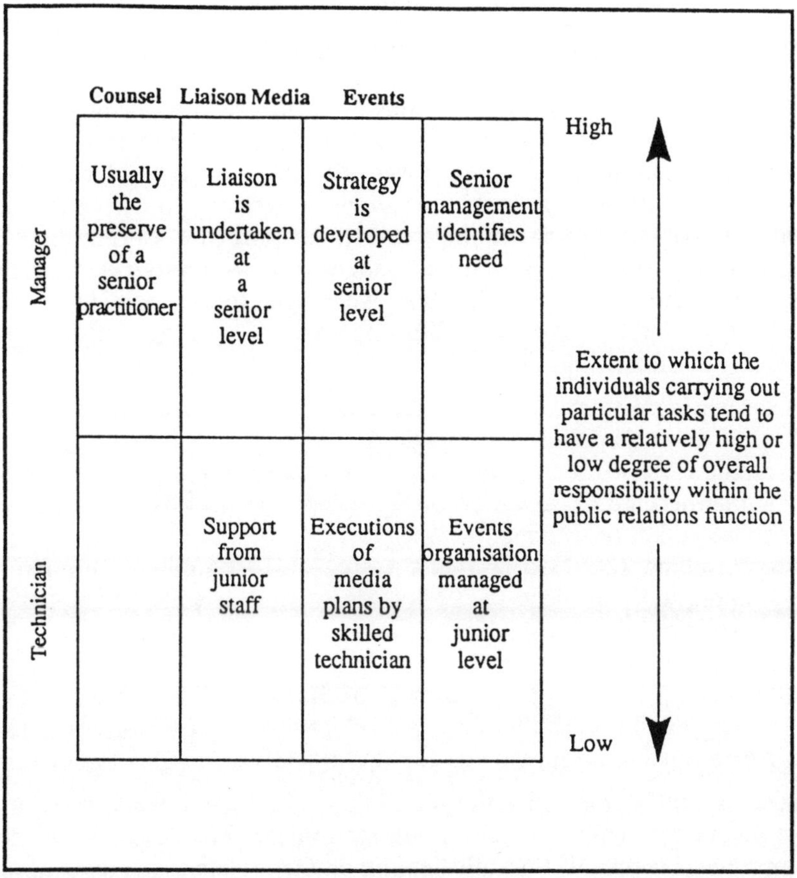

	Counsel	Liaison Media		Events	
Manager	Usually the preserve of a senior practitioner	Liaison is undertaken at a senior level	Strategy is developed at senior level	Senior management identifies need	High ↑
					Extent to which the individuals carrying out particular tasks tend to have a relatively high or low degree of overall responsibility within the public relations function
Technician		Support from junior staff	Executions of media plans by skilled technician	Events organisation managed at junior level	Low ↓

Figure 6.1 *Illustrating the different levels of tasks in a typical public relations programme*

Canon

Canon prepared a public relations programme to support its marketing of the company's photocopiers. The schedule included the following:

- technical, trade and business media relations;
- football sponsorship;
- mounting exhibition stands at trade and consumer events;
- designing and producing new literature;
- organising dealer competitions with prizes;

- advertising and direct mail. (These last items might appear to be outside public relations but their style has to be in conformity with overall public relations policy).

The Barbican Arts and Conference Centre, London

The Barbican project presented unusual factors as it was conceived in 1956 but only begun in earnest in 1970. The design and construction phase lasted about 10 years and it was officially opened by Her Majesty the Queen in 1982. The public relations programme thus began with spreading an awareness of the project, keeping the Corporation of London supportive, interesting the residents who were suffering from the noise and dirt of the construction work and finally publicising the availability of the Centre's facilities for hire. The range of activities included the following:

- discussing with the architects the ways in which the centre would be used for conferences and meetings;
- media relations on a local, national and international scale;
- a planned programme of press receptions and facility visits as construction proceeded;
- counselling the Corporation's responsible committees on issues relating to the project;
- production of descriptive brochures and the publication of a regular newsletter;
- arranging visits by VIPs to the site of the developing centre;
- promoting the facilities of the centre at suitable exhibitions overseas;
- preparing the arrangements for the official opening of the Centre.

These examples emphasize the wide range of activities which may form part of typical public relations programmes. The success of any comprehensive plan will usually depend on the effective execution of the constituent parts and meticulous attention to detail is essential if the overall plan is to succeed.

Having explained how many different activities come together to form a complete programme, it is time to discuss some of these constituent parts.

The printed word

The spoken word was undoubtedly the first organized method of communication, but it was overtaken by the printed word when printing methods were invented and in due course became widely available. Despite the introduction of radio and television, the printed word remains the most important medium of communication. We use the term to include illustrations and graphics.

The print output of a typical company will cover a wide range of items, both for external and internal consumption. Invoices, forms, letterheadings and similar printed matter might appear to have little in common with annual reports or house journals but it is very desirable that all printed matter of a company should have a family resemblance. Whatever procedures are in place for ordering printed matter, the question of style and design should remain a public relations responsibility.

Style, design and typography

Fashions in typography and print design change radically as time passes, as can be seen easily by reading a newspaper or magazine published ten years ago. Television programmes also accustom people to modern typography and it is a mistake to believe that the general public are not influenced by good design.

This book is not the place for a detailed discussion on typography, but there is a definite public relations aspect of print style and design. Legibility should always be the first consideration, for the whole purpose of print is to encourage reading and this should be made as easy and as enticing as possible. This is not to suggest that everything should be dull and commonplace. Interesting lay-out and relevant illustrations are very desirable but legibility should always be the most important criterion. The modern fad of printing in grey instead of black is to be deprecated.

Comparison of a typical annual report or company newsletter with similar items published ten years ago shows how the influence of enlightened public relations men and women has improved the interest of the report and the legibility of corporate print. The use of colour has become firmly established, except where cost is the major consideration, but colour should be used intelligently and not employed just to give a pretty effect. When the production of print is left entirely to a designer, the result is sometimes idiosyncratic, like the use of blue type on a dark blue background which looks artistic but makes reading very difficult. This kind of error will be avoided if the prime importance of easy legibility is always borne in mind.

A new development, which is also to be deprecated, is the fairly common habit of using very small print. This results from the widespread use of type production by computer and the temptation to get as much text as possible into a circumscribed area. This is a particularly bad mistake, especially when the text is intended for reading by middle-aged or elderly people who are likely to have problems reading small print.

There is a constant optimum relationship between the length of a column of type and its legibility. The use of two or three columns on a magazine page is not affectation, but recognition of the importance of readability of the page in question. There is no suggestion that all printed items should be designed in a uniform or boring style, but in designing and producing any type of printed matter the consideration of easy legibility should always be a priority.

Working with the printer

Despite the increasing use of desktop publishing for in-house printing of many items, even perhaps including house journals, there will be many occasions when conventional printing will be required.

In order to secure good service from a printer, it is desirable to acquire a working knowledge of printing methods and techniques and some familiarity with the jargon. Without this background understanding, it may be difficult to discuss intelligently the different possibilities and to be able to assess the proposals of designers or typographers. Printers prefer to work with clients who have a working familiarity with printing techniques and modern production methods.

There are three important factors in commissioning printed work of any kind: cost, service and the quality of the finished work. In general, one gets the service and quality of the finished work that one is prepared to pay for. It is worth remembering, however, that printers fall into different categories, depending on their resources in machinery and skilled operatives. The best printers have efficient proof readers, smaller firms do not.

The question of service covers a number of different considerations. It is very helpful if it is possible to contact the printer quickly and if at times they are willing to do the impossible in speedy production.

The question of security may also be a factor in choosing a printer, particularly for financial documents which are likely to be subject to Stock Exchange or other controls.

Few companies employ their own typographer, so it is customary to use the services of a freelance designer or a company providing a design service. Often one employs a number of different designers to achieve variety of approach. An experienced typographer will be an expert on design but many have different ideas from the public relations practitioner who should know the final effect he or she is aiming to achieve.

Apart from typography and design, a good or bad impression can result from the choice of materials. Good examples of print may be spoilt by unwise choice of paper. A company reporting a substantial loss in its annual report should exercise restraint in its production — not too utilitarian, however, as this might spread alarm. Likewise a national charity appealing for funds should avoid the use of too expensive paper and presentation.

The appearance of a piece of print conveys a silent message, good or bad, quite separate from the actual words or pictures. There is a public relations aspect of a printed item which results from the correct level of sophistication.

Desktop publishing

The introduction of computers into normal office routine has brought with it the possibility of printing in-house a wide variety of printed matter with good definition. The essential hardware consists of a powerful computer, a monitor, a scanner and a good printer. Bubble jet printers are now available which give excellent results at a much lower cost than laser printers. Using appropriate software packages, high definition print can be produced in-house, with a wide variety of type sizes and fonts and layout possibilities.

The production of newsletters, brochures, information leaflets, office stationery and even annual reports can be achieved but the results are likely to be very disappointing unless the operator has considerable typographical and design skills, coupled with wide experience and familiarity with the equipment. It is easy to produce printed matter with desktop publishing, but difficult to produce really satisfactory results.

There are two reasons for using desktop publishing: convenience and economy. It is certainly very useful to be able to produce print at very short notice but the economy is somewhat doubtful if full allowance is made for the time factor involved. Another positive factor can be security: there is less danger of leaks when the work is carried out on the premises.

The art of writing

Choosing a good printer is very important in communicating by the printed word, but it is even more important to ensure that the quality of the text is appropriate and well written. Many books have been published giving advice on business English, or the preparation of reports, or writing novels, but little has been published giving advice on writing for public relations.

Since the primary object of any written communication is to impart information, it is obviously desirable that the text should be unambiguous and easy to understand. Convoluted writing may be fine in novels but should have no place in the use of the printed word for clear communication.

The British Civil Service used to have the unenviable reputation of using complicated expressions and very involved sentences. Sir Edward Gowers was invited to give guidance to civil servants on this subject and this resulted in his two classic books: *Plain Words* and the *ABC of Plain Words*, both of which are still worth careful study. There is no suggestion that we should emulate the French writer, Flaubert who was reputed to spend hours, or even days, to get a word or a sentence polished to his complete satisfaction. Gowers counselled thus: 'The article you are paid to produce need not be polished but it must be workmanlike'. Without becoming too pedantic, it is desirable to aim at preserving the use of correct language which is such an important medium of public relations.

Excellent advice is given by *The Economist* to its correspondents. They are advised to use Anglo-Saxon instead of Latin words. The following preferences are quoted: About *not* approximately; after *not* follow; let *not* permit; but *not* however; use *not* utilize; make *not* manufacture; plant *not* facility; take part *not* participate; set up *not* establish; enough *not* sufficient; show *not* demonstrate, and so on. Underdeveloped countries are often better described as poor; substantive usually means real or big. To this excellent advice, can be added some personal hates: 'gone missing', and the incorrect use of 'decimate' and 'anticipate'. . . .

The KISS rule is a good system to follow in both speaking and writing. Keep It Short and Simple. This means using short sentences and making statements logically and simple and free from clichés and mixed metaphors.

House journals

There are a number of different types of publications which are produced for public relations purposes. Of these, the most important are house journals which are of two main types: internal and external. As the names indicate, the former are for reading within the organization, while external publications are intended mainly for an outside readership.

The title 'house journal' has superseded the earlier and more correct title 'house magazine' even though few, if any, are published 'daily'. It has been estimated that in Britain there are nearly 2000 publications of this kind, with a total circulation of 23 million at an annual cost of £15 million — obviously this remains a preferred form of internal public relations.

A house journal is usually defined as 'a non-profit making periodical published by an organization to establish or maintain contact with its employees or sections of the public'. As with any type of publication, a house journal must be planned so as best to meet its objectives. The main reason for producing an internal house journal is to provide a communication link with employees. An external publication has a different function. Its main objective is to make contact with groups and individuals outside the organization with the aim of improving reputation and encouraging various kinds of cooperation. It is fairly obvious that the requirements of the two different readerships make it very difficult to satisfy these disparate interests within one journal. Apart from editorial difficulties, the economic realities make it difficult, if not impossible, to produce a successful internal/external house journal.

Internal house journals

Publications designed for internal readership are usually published in newspaper format. This gives the journal a sense of immediacy by association with the newspapers that are familiar reading. It is easy to produce and comparatively inexpensive. Many of these house journals are now produced in-house by using desktop publishing. Two typical newsletters are the *Vauxhall Mirror* and *Cover* published by Vauxhall Motors at Luton and by ICI Paints: The content of these two publications is quite different but the presentation and editorial policy is rather similar. The format and page size resemble a tabloid newspaper and the 12 pages are full of excellent colour pictures. Both journals have a mix of company news and stories about employees and their activities. These well-designed colourful glossy publications are typical of newsletters published in the UK by large organizations. They have come a long way from the more rudimentary internal communications that served as house journals in the past. Whether the new glossies are better at communicating than their earlier forerunners is open to question.

With internal house journals it is important to bear in mind why they are published. The primary objective is communication between management and employees in order to keep them informed and happy in their work. To this end, the main requirement is to present the news and features in a way that will encourage employees to read the papers and take them home for their families' interest.

There are two elements to the production of any internal house journal:

- how to produce it so that it will not be too expensive; and
- how to ensure its contents will hold the interest of readers and make them look forward with keen anticipation to the next issue.

It is important to bear in mind that too much management emphasis in a journal will kill any idea that it is published for the benefit of employees. One way in which this problem manifests itself is the number of times the journal carries the photograph and message of the chairman or chief executive officer. A personal view is that this should be kept to a minimum, perhaps once a year unless there are exceptional circumstances. The Vauxhall newspaper has an interesting variant on this point. The chairman of the company has a series of meetings with groups of employees and the questions and answers from these meetings are featured in the newsletters. This is ingenious as it provides a way of including company policy without it appearing to be dictatorial.

To sum up, it is inevitable that the quality and presentation of internal house journals will tend to keep up with modern expectations but their most important aspect is the content, not the presentation.

There are a number of policy decisions which have to be taken in connection with publishing internal house journals. How will they be distributed; will there be a charge to employees; should outside advertising be accepted to reduce the overall cost; to what extent should employees be allowed to voice criticism of the management? There is plenty of room for disagreement on these and similar questions. On distribution, the size of the company will be a major consideration. Delivery to the point of work or at the factory gate is perhaps the most usual method. Some companies, however, prefer to post copies to employees' homes despite the extra cost, in the hope that families will also be exposed to the journal contents.

External house journals

It is even more difficult to attract and interest readers of external house journals. The type and style of external house journals varies greatly but most of them are published in magazine format resembling typical magazines which are sold in shops or — increasingly — distributed free. Communication is again the main reason for publication, but the quality of photographs and editorial content are of much greater importance as the objective is to reach and interest an uncommitted readership.

This field of publishing is expanding rapidly. In addition to publications intended for suppliers or customers, there are many well-produced magazines distributed by airlines and hotel groups. A difference here is that they include a substantial number of advertisements aimed at the captive readership. The main objective of publication is, however, to establish contact and to enhance reputation leading to increased profitability.

Photography in public relations

In media relations and house journals, annual reports and other publications, illustrations and photographs have an important part to play, but there are also other uses of photography in public relations. There are five main uses:

1. In media relations, to illustrate news releases which are sent to newspapers or trade and technical journals.
2. For use as illustrations in house journals, annual reports or other company publications.
3. For use at exhibitions or in advertisements or posters.

4. For training and research.
5. For record purposes.

Photographs for news stories must be topical, striking and interesting and adequately captioned. Every picture must tell a story if it is likely to be used. If you are inviting the press to take photographs at a news conference, it is usually advisable to have a photocall immediately prior to the main conference.

For use in advertisements or at exhibitions, a different approach is required, The photographs will probably be used in colour and there is more time to plan and take the pictures. When photographs are commissioned for training or research or for record purposes, the requirements again are quite different and exact detail and scale are probably important.

Good photographers will achieve satisfactory results even under adverse conditions but it is advantageous to take some trouble to help the photographer achieve optimum results. Take care about copyright of photographs taken for you. The copyright in photographs specially commissioned from a photographer belongs to the client. The copyright in photographs taken by a photographer and offered for sale remain with the photographer and not with the purchaser. Unless otherwise agreed, the negatives are retained by the photographer.

It is tempting these days to take one's own photographs but if they are required for professional use it is wise to employ the best photographer that can be afforded.

The spoken word

Expansion of radio and television have accentuated the importance of the spoken word as a means of communication. Some people have the ability to speak with confidence on any occasion, but other less fortunate people have to develop this facility. Some of the world's best orators have not been born with the gift, but have had to develop it by hard work. Courses are available at speech training schools where it is possible to acquire confidence and to learn how to make the best impression when called upon to deliver a speech or to be interviewed. There should not be any embarrassment for a senior executive to take this opportunity of improving his or her skill as a speaker. Using a video recording of a speech rehearsal can be effective in revealing unfortunate mannerisms or habits such as rocking backwards and forwards or excessive blinking. A short course at a speech training school can soon eliminate these unhelpful habits.

Apart from writing speeches when required, a public relations practitioner can do much to help a speaker. Microphones should always be tested in advance and adjusted for height. The lectern should be placed in the most suitable location and always fitted with a reading light. If visual aids are to be used, such as an overhead projector, slides or videos, the equipment should be tested in advance and an operator should be briefed adequately.

A good speech can have a very powerful effect, possibly more than any other single form of communication, so it is worth a considerable effort to ensure that the right speech is delivered on the most appropriate occasion by the best orator available.

Exhibitions and conferences

It is logical to discuss exhibitions, trade fairs and conferences together as it has become usual for exhibitions to complement conferences and vice versa. The reason for this is because it increases the attendance at both events and helps to make the conferences financially viable.

Organizers of conferences with supporting exhibitions must arrange the two events so that it is possible for those attending the conference to visit the exhibits. Both the conference and the exhibition should be held in the same building and the conference programme should allow ample time for visiting the exhibition.

This subject of exhibitions covers a wide variety of events designed to bring together individuals or organizations desirous of discussing matters of mutual interest and sharing ideas or developing business connections. Participation in an exhibition may well depend on marketing policy and production schedules, but the planning and organization of the stand is usually a public relations responsibility.

Exhibitions range from huge world events such as the 1992 World Fair in Seville to small displays of products or ideas to a small invited audience. World fairs are usually the concern of countries, but there may be opportunity for some involvement by commerce and industry. In every instance. the choice of exhibits and their design and presentation should be audience led. In other words, the objectives of taking part in an event should always be the determining factors.

Choosing exhibitions to support

So many exhibitions are held each year, both at home and overseas, that the selection of suitable events to support may be very difficult. In some industries, the regular support of certain events may be obvious but outside these priority exhibitions there is a bewildering number of events from which to choose. In considering participation at a new event, it is necessary to ascertain the exact scope of the exhibition, the size of the expected attendance and the likely proportion of buyers. It is usually difficult to assess the value of an event until it has been running for some years so many companies avoid participation in new events. The best way to evaluate an exhibition is by supplementing the data provided by the organizers with a personal visit.

Planning participation

Except at large prestige shows, it has become usual to accept the shell schemes offered by the exhibition organizers. Shell schemes began as a series of egg-crate like areas which were supplied complete with fascia, floor covering and minimal lighting. This rudimentary idea has blossomed into well-designed shells which can be adapted to make very acceptable stands with a minimum of stand fitting and cost. It is usually possible to be able to combine a number of neighbouring areas to provide quite large stands.

Unless the stand is to be quite small, it is wise to brief a designer with experience of exhibition design. He or she will require a detailed brief, setting out the objectives of participation, the products to be shown and the size of the stand. Armed with this information, the designer can suggest ways of making the maximum impact. The designer's responsibilities include assistance in seeking tenders for the stand construction and supervising the erection and completion of the stand. For detailed information on this subject, the reader is referred to *Exhibitions and conferences from A to Z* by Sam Black (Modino Press, 1989).

When the design has been accepted and the contractor appointed, there are many other matters that require careful attention. The exhibition organizers will usually provide a book of application forms for ordering furniture, cleaning and other additional services. Transport for the exhibits and travel and accommodation for the staff require early attention. Insurance must be arranged and literature to be handed out at the exhibition must be ordered in good time. If the show is overseas, translation is likely to be needed and care is essential to ensure correct texts. This is not as easy as one might expect, particularly when dealing with lesser known languages like Hungarian, Finnish or Bahasa. A good tip is to have the translation checked in the country in which it will be used. This may seem to be exaggerating the problem but most exporters can tell tragic stories of mis-translation.

It is desirable to plan carefully how the stand will be manned. If the hours of opening are long it is likely to be necessary to arrange rotas. Efficient staffing of an exhibition stand is essential if all enquiries are to be logged accurately so that they can be followed up in an attempt to convert enquiries into firm orders.

This is not the place to discuss the minutiae of stand design, but one point is worth emphasizing. By clever design and arrangement, a stand can attract visitors into a stand, while those which are poorly designed can form a real barrier between the visitors and the staff waiting to answer queries.

Dealing with enquiries

There are two main objectives in participating in an exhibition or trade fair.

1. **Public relations**. Taking part in a satisfactory manner protects reputation and provides an opportunity of meeting existing customers and contacts or making new ones. There are also other public relations activities which can be based on the company's presence in the exhibition or trade fair.

2. **To take orders or receive enquiries**. These can, hopefully, be converted into orders in due course. It is obvious that careful attention to the receipt and handling of enquiries is very important. There is skill, usually gained from experience, in being able to differentiate between serious and casual enquiries.

Sponsorship

Sponsorship is a comparatively new medium of public relations which allows companies to communicate with audiences that are difficult to contact by normal marketing methods.

Sponsorship deals should be based on sound commercial considerations. A useful definition of sponsorship insists that it must be of benefit to both the sponsor and the sponsored. While sponsorship can be regarded as part of the marketing mix, it may have a direct effect on the company's corporate image so its style and choice of subject should be integrated with the overall public relations policy.

Sport and the arts sponsorship are probably the most visible examples but nine different types of sponsorship can be identified:

1. **Sport**. The largest part of the sponsor's money goes to sport. This includes test cricket, league football, motor racing, snooker, cycle racing, tennis, show jumping, athletics and many other kinds of sport at national and local level.

2. **Arts and culture**. Sponsors support the ballet, opera, the theatre, classical and rock concerts, art exhibitions and many individual artistic ventures.

3. **Exhibitions** have been sponsored for many years and the national newspapers are particularly active in this field. The *Daily Mail Ideal*

Home Exhibition has long been a fixture in London in March each year.

4. **Books**. Sponsors produce books, such as the *Guinness Book of Records*, the *Michelin Guide*, or give prizes for the best books, such as the Booker Prize.

5. **Education**. Chairs at universities, scholarships, fellowships and research projects are some of the ways in which assistance is provided in the academic and educational fields.

6. **Charities and good causes**. Help in this respect may be anonymous but there are many occasions where credits are given.

7. **Professional awards**. Sponsored awards are offered for many different kinds of achievement in the professions, the arts or social or community service.

8. **Expeditions**. This category covers support for exploration, archaeology, mountain climbing and many other expeditions, large or small.

9. **Local sponsorship**. These early examples of sponsorship have long been the recipients of support from industry. They include local festivals, carnivals, flower shows, swimming galas and similar local events.

The Association for Business Sponsorship of the Arts

This association was formed to encourage companies to spend more on sponsoring the arts in Britain and its efforts have been of very great assistance. Since 1978, awards have been given annually to highlight the best examples of arts sponsorship. These ABSA/Arthur Andersen awards now invite nominations in ten different categories and over 400 entries are received each year.

Sponsorship has been a life support for a place like the Royal Academy of Arts which receives no grant from the Arts Council or any other official body. The Academy has pioneered an innovative system of underwriting for its major exhibitions. The sponsor guarantees to cover the net cost (after deducting receipts from entrance fees and catalogue sales) up to an agreed maximum. Some lucky sponsors have not had to pay anything.

Measuring results of sponsorship

Sponsorship is not altruism, so it is important to plan participation on the basis of likely benefits to accrue to the sponsor who provides the money.

It is very desirable for a company to sponsor events which have some affinity to its products or major interests and to select those which are likely to appeal to the same people who buy the sponsor's products or services. Much of the benefits of sponsorship come from the signs which will be seen on television: this is particularly true of football and cricket matches. The selection of positions for signs is important and should be negotiated in advance.

Deciding to sponsor an event should not be a sudden whim but needs careful advance planning. In particular, sponsors should decide which audiences they wish to reach and influence. A sponsor of suitable events may be able to use them as appropriate occasions at which to offer hospitality to customers or potential clients.

Efforts should be made to measure the results of money spent on sponsorship. Quantitative assessment may be difficult, but research can establish the extent to which money spent on sponsorship has increased company visibility, enhanced reputation and aided profitability.

Lobbying and parliamentary liaison

There has been considerable controversy as to whether or not lobbying is a legitimate part of public relations. Lobbying, if carried out honestly, is an important part of parliamentary liaison and has an essential part to play in many public relations programmes.

Lobbying is an accepted part of the democratic process and its nature is determined by the type of parliamentary and political system. Most public relations practitioners choose to leave lobbying to the growing number of men and women who specialize in this complex field. A recent report highlighted the amount of 'uncontrolled and uncoordinated' lobbying which is claimed to be costing British business over £100 million a year by failing to provide a fully professional service. The British political system relies heavily on consultation, but this degree of consultation may be quite limited if many businesses, trade associations, trade unions, public bodies and other interested organizations fail to ensure that their point of view will be taken into consideration.

The civil servants in Whitehall, MPs and peers in the Houses of Parliament, MEPs and officials in the European Commission at Brussels and Strasbourg all need to be made aware of the possible adverse consequences of their proposed decisions. Informing civil servants and politicians about the impact of proposed legislation is not merely enlightened self-interest, but is a vital part of the democratic process. Lobbying is legitimate and to be welcomed, provided it conforms to accepted codes of conduct.

Lobbying should always be carried out in a sophisticated manner and it usually has three essential elements: intelligence, communication and pressure.

1. **Intelligence** gives early warning of problems or opportunities. It provides the essential background on which to form strategy and

tactics. It is necessary to identify likely allies and enemies and the timescale is very critical.

2. **Communication** implies the opportunity to transmit the message in the best form, to the ideal audience at the right time.
3. **Pressure** ensures that necessary actions will be taken by the right people on the most effective timescale and with consistency.

To succeed at lobbying, it is necessary to have the patience to listen, the ability to communicate complex messages, coupled with determination and courage.

Lobbying in the European Community

The process of decision-making in Brussels is very different from that in Westminster and Whitehall. In the UK, there is plenty of advance notice of forthcoming legislation: in the Queen's speech, election manifestos, white papers and exhaustive coverage in the media. It is much more difficult to find out what is happening in Brussels or Strasbourg, or what is likely to be coming up for discussion. There is a steady stream of directives coming out of Brussels which can affect materially the future of British companies. An organization can make its own representations at Brussels but it is more cost-effective, and probably more successful, to use an experienced lobbyist.

The Commission is much less secretive than Whitehall. It is open to questions, suggestions or advice because officials there prefer to introduce legislation which will not arouse too much opposition.

A collective voice carries more weight at Brussels than that of a single national point of view so it is very useful to try to achieve cooperation with your opposite numbers in other EC countries so that collective action can be taken. In the private sector, companies who are normally competitors can often jointly influence Brussels.

Any case to be presented to the Commission must be carefully prepared in advance and if it appears to be reasonable it is more likely to receive a good reception. Time is of the essence. It is essential to keep well informed and apprised of sensitive proposals as long in advance as possible. Many good opportunities are lost by failure to act soon enough. In general, the complex nature of the European Community makes it a veritable minefield except for the most experienced lobbyist.

Much of the criticism about lobbying centres round the use of MPs or MEPs by some public relations companies to work on lobbying. At Brussels, the European Parliament's rules committee has been considering draft regulations for the control of lobbying by MEPs. The draft includes a provision that MEPs should be forced to register all their financial interests and to update them annually. The public register would be held in Brussels but copies of it would be available in all member states.

7
Corporate identity and visual communication

The Royal Society of Arts and the Design Council have worked very hard and consistently to encourage a greater appreciation by British industry of the importance of industrial design. Good design should permeate throughout a company's activities as it will bring good dividends in profitability and internal morale. Good design does not just happen. It requires a positive commitment from top management, but the responsibility for monitoring this vital aspect of the organization rests squarely with the public relations advisers.

According to Laszlo Moholy Nagy (Bauhaus member from 1922 until his death in 1946), 'Design is an attitude of mind, a search for perfection in an imperfect world'.

The effective use of design, of which corporate identity programmes are a part, can undoubtedly help a company to gain and sustain competitive advantage. In his book *Corporate Identity*, Wally Olins uses the sub-title 'making business strategy visible through design'. This statement is true of the use of good design in every aspect of business but does not apply only to corporate identity. Olins and other designers specializing in corporate identity often refer to their work as corporate communication. This is true, but very confusing as there are many other constituent parts of corporate communication. Public relations is the only term which describes the comprehensive field of corporate communication of which corporate identity is a part.

In the UK, as in most other industrialized countries, there is a steadily growing interest in corporate identity and corporate image but these two terms, which are not synonymous, are often confused. Corporate *image* is how the public perceives a company. Fowler, in *Modern English Usage*, explains the meaning of the word 'image' as the 'idea — the general impression — of some person or institution received by the mind's eye of an outsider, and the image received will determine whether the person or institution is good or bad'. Corporate *identity*, on the other hand, is the composite personality of the company derived from its philosophy, history, culture, strategies, management style, reputation, and the behaviour of employees, salesmen and other company representatives. Like a person, a company develops a perceived character and builds up a certain reputation in the minds of others. A company is recognized by the outward and visible manifestations of many attributes, and it is the visual aspects of these which are likely to be exposed to public scrutiny more continuously than other forms of communication.

The reputation of any company will always depend, in the first place, on the quality of its performance and the products or services provided.

Objectives of corporate identity

Every corporate body has many points of contact with a wide variety of people, though the areas of contact will differ widely. A company has premises and environments of varying kinds. It has works, products, packaging, stationery, forms, vehicles, uniforms or protective clothing, signposting requirements, publications and many kinds of promotional activities. These features are seen by the company's customers, suppliers, shareholders, agents, the media and the general public as well as by its own staff and employees. The people in these groups build up their idea of the company by what they experience and see of it. It follows that the coordination of all the visual characteristics of these areas of influence to a planned, consistent and appropriate design standard, must play a vital part in establishing a favourable concept of a company's standing in the minds of the public it serves. This applies also in the minds of its markets, in the minds of its employees and in the minds of potential investors.

The adoption of a planned corporate identity programme represents something more than merely a company's faith in its own service to the public. It encourages among the company's staff a feeling that they are working for a progressive organization, builds morale and helps to recruit and retain staff.

A public relations strategy for a company must therefore take into account many considerations and although an appropriate corporate identity will be an important aspect, it must be an integrated part of the whole personality of the company and not an end in itself.

Benefits

The benefits of a successful corporate identity programme are likely to include both direct and indirect selling advantages, promotional advantages, and an improved financial standing. But the prime reason for the adoption and implementation of a visual corporate identity programme lies in its commercial value and its contribution to net revenue. A MORI opinion poll revealed that people consistently prefer to buy from firms with a known name. For example, 61 per cent of housewives were prepared to try a new frozen food when testers stated that it was made by Heinz, but when the testers stated instead that it was made by a large (unnamed) food company, the proportion dropped to 47 per cent. Many other surveys confirm that most people buy on the strength of reputation.

Corporate identity was earlier referred to as house style. Milner Gray, CBE, RDI, the doyen of corporate design, recalls how ICI stated:

> The main justification for a house style is its potential commercial value. One of the basic requirements of good marketing is to have a clearly identifiable product, emanating from an equally well recognizable source. Properly conceived and implemented, a house style adds the additional dimension of coherence to the image which a company projects. The elements of design, colour, lettering and symbol — used consistently — combine to create a memorable overall impression. Lack of a consistent house style, on the other hand, can be damaging to a company's public image: as well as creating an impression of archaism, incoherency and muddle: it can detract from an otherwise good marketing organization.

The faith of ICI in corporate identity has been emphasized by its recent updating of its logo and corporate identity. With the announcement by the company that ICI is splitting into two separate bodies, it will be very interesting to see how this will affect its logo. Figure 7.1 shows how the new ICI logo has evolved.

Another organization which has demonstrated its belief in corporate identity is British Rail. A former chairman of British Rail wrote:

> The future of British Railways depends upon what the travelling public and industry think of them, and to create the right public impression we have to provide good service and also present an appearance of smartness and efficiency. Neither is a substitute for the other — both are necessary. The best way of creating the right visual impression of an organization as widespread as ours is the consistent use of the same well designed distinguishing features wherever they can appropriately be embodied. This gives cumulative impact to the features used, causes the organization's facilities to be easily recognized, and produces a corporate identity which reflects the unity of the organization behind all our activities.

The moral of British Rail's current problems is that while corporate identity can make an important contribution to an organization's success it is no substitute whatsoever for adequate capital investment. With the forthcoming privatization of British Rail, its corporate identity policy is presumably due for a radical shake up.

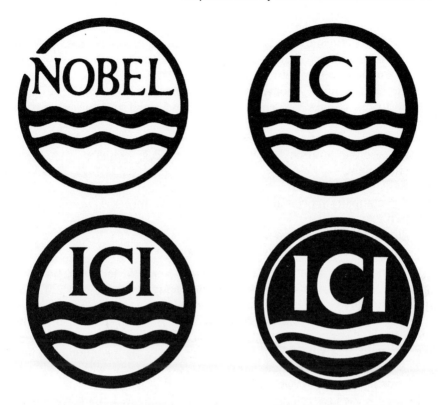

Figure 7.1 *An example of how a new logo has developed from earlier patterns*

The initiation of a corporate identity programme frequently results in benefits over and above the obvious external and internal promotional gains. The planning of such a programme necessitates the study of every operation which may have a visual impact on any section of the public — with the aim of coordinating the design of each item. This tends to lead, by simplification and standardization of items, to a reduction of unnecessary varieties, and by a process of rationalization, to long-term economies in production and maintenance systems and costs.

In order to achieve the full benefit of a successful corporate identity programme, the company must first undertake the appropriate research to define the organization's present and projected identity. Corporate identities should not be changed on a whim and before a change is contemplated, comprehensive research is essential.

The scope of a corporate identity programme

The visual manifestations of a company can cover a wide variety of different items:

- the corporate name;
- the logo (lettering, typography, and possibly a graphic rearrangement of the name);
- an emblem or symbol;
- the house colour scheme;
- uniforms, badges, protective clothing and ancillary equipment such as flags;
- characteristics of a company's products;
- the architectural style of factories, offices, vehicles and other equipment;
- signs and directional information (indoors and outside);
- the company's printed matter (stationery, forms, advertisements, publicity matter);
- displays and exhibition stands;
- films, videos and audio-visual material.

Not every organization will need to consider all these items, but it is important to remember that all relevant items will have a positive or negative influence.

Every company has an image in the minds of the public, but how memorable, distinctive, accurate, positive and deliberate it is depends on the thoroughness with which the peculiar problems have been studied and assessed by the design consultant and the skill with which the solutions have been devised and implemented.

Normally the basic elements of corporate design are a mark or symbol, a name style and letter form, a house colour or series of colours. Once a decision has been made to design, re-design or develop a company's identity, clear management decisions and controls are required. Top management must take full responsibility and approve the *modus operandi*. Once the basic management decisions have been taken, delegation must follow, both inside and outside the company.

A practical method of procedure is to have a small working party — not more than six persons — half from the company and the other half from the design consultant's staff. The public relations adviser will normally take the lead for the company. The designers will ask for information and guidance as the work develops. Finally, the agreed basic design solution will be presented as a team proposal. Management then has the right of acceptance or may ask for modifications. Outright rejection is unlikely if all the preliminary stages have been carried out systematically.

Areas which require examination and decision

The following areas require careful examination and decision:

- **Objectives**: to agree ultimate goals and prepare the basis of the design brief.

- **Research**: to determine what information is needed to establish the parameters of the design study and to decide who will research it if this does not exist.
- **Project planning**: to establish scope, time span and cost dimension.
- **Appointment of designers**: internal or external — if outside, establish the role of the public relations staff and other internal executives.
- **Interpretation and application**: which design elements will become mandatory, which discretionary — what manuals, master drawings, colour samples and guidance material will be required?
- **Organization**: what internal organizational machinery and procedures will be required?
- **Communications**: what steps will be taken to publicize the new identity to middle management, employees, shareholders, the target publics, the public at large and outside agencies?
- **Evaluation**: establishing a system for periodic review during the design development stages and continued monitoring after implementation.

These eight development stages are a useful check list which can be adjusted to individual needs.

A quote from a boardroom

Milner Gray has quoted a Board decision which established the basic objectives and procedures for initiating a new corporate identity programme. This stated:

As we are predominantly a service institution without visible products or packages, we have always needed and shall always need distinctive visual recognition of our service facilities and materials involved in giving our services: our branch offices, signs, printed forms, stationery, publicity materials, etc. These materials do carry at present a fairly consistent house style. But we believe, and this has been reinforced by recent research reports, that this style is out-of-date and might help to give the wrong impression to potential customers.

In broad terms, our redefined image aims are as follows:

1. We wish to be seen as a large, leading, reliable, trustworthy financial service institution, well established and highly experienced. We believe that we are indeed seen in these terms already. We do not wish to lose this aspect of our profile which has made us what we are,
2. However, we must now prove to be more acceptable to new social classes and age groups. We have to appear to them, within reason and

without losing continuity of our established profile, more forward-looking, more human, warmer, more accessible, less forbidding, more lively, more flexible and dynamic.

3. We have decided to undertake a number of long-term programmes to achieve this: staff training, service development, advertising, public relations and a new 'corporate identity'.

This example is quoted in some detail as it illustrates the thinking at board level which appreciated the factors dictating the reasons for a new corporate identity programme, and understood that it must be supported by staff training and positive public relations.

Some thoughts on logos

It has been emphasized that a new corporate identity involves many different factors, but the adopted logo (or symbol) and logotype will always be the factor that attracts most public notice.

It is always very difficult to obtain agreement from a committee on the choice of a new logo, but there are a number of elements which should help to achieve a consensus. A successful logo will be distinctive, memorable, pleasing to the eye and, if possible, have a direct relation to the company or its activities. It must be amenable to use in many different sizes and in different circumstances with equally good effect. A personal view is that the best logos are very simple, quite different from all other logos and possessing instant recognizability. The Shell logo is an excellent example.

A new development has been complementing a logo with an accompanying slogan. Recent examples are:

ICI — Solving world problems — world class;
BP — For all our tomorrows;
BT — You talk, we listen and together we'll build the future;
Ford — Everything we do is driven by you.

Evolution of a logo

Some of the best logos have come about by evolution, not by a completely new design. A good example of this is the way in which Vauxhall Motors Limited have followed tradition in the redesign of their corporate identity programme.

In launching the new programme, the company explained that it was eliminating the confusion of marques, badges and logos that had accumulated during the 1980s and was replacing them with a new and distinctive motif that would focus clearly on 'Vauxhall' as the corporate name and brand identity. Historically, there had been separate badging for Vauxhall cars and Bedford vans. Further, dealer premises displayed multiple signs showing Vauxhall-Opel-Bedford-GM, a throwback to the amalgamation of the Vauxhall and Opel dealer networks in the early 1980s. The Opel marque is no longer sold in the UK. With the concurrent announcement that Bedford vans were now to be badged 'Vauxhall', the unification of brand identity had been completed. The new logo will still be supported by the General Motors corporate logo when appropriate in some business settings.

Vauxhall commissioned Wolff Olins to research the whole area of the company's corporate identity, over a period of 12 months. The result is a new logo and livery that is being applied uniformly across everything associated with Vauxhall, from stationery to transport fleet and buildings. Most significant will be the progressive signing of all 630 Vauxhall dealerships nationwide, which will also include new interior designs to make the facilities truly customer-focused centres. Showrooms will better reflect the design, quality and market success of Vauxhall products. Exteriors of dealer premises will feature the new green-grey livery.

Vauxhall's griffin symbol was inherited from the Vauxhall Iron Works, founded in 1857. The logo has evolved progressively since the present company was formed in 1907. Through more than eight decades, the griffin — stylized according to the taste of the period — has formed the basis of the company's trademark. That tradition is continuing in the new style and culture of Vauxhall. Figure 7.2 shows the development of the Griffin symbol from the 1920s to the 1990s.

Designing and maintaining a house style

Whether a logo and house style evolve or are newly designed, it is essential to have firm rules which will ensure the integrity of the design and will prevent it becoming spoilt by misuse. To this end, it is necessary to produce a rule book or corporate identity manual which describes in considerable detail:

- the colour(s) to be used;
- the symbol;
- the logotype; and
- the ways in which these items may be used singly or together.

The book usually includes examples of inadmissible ways of using the elements of the new corporate identity.

The Honda Motor Company is a good example of this treatment. They have published a *Basic System* book which describes in very great detail

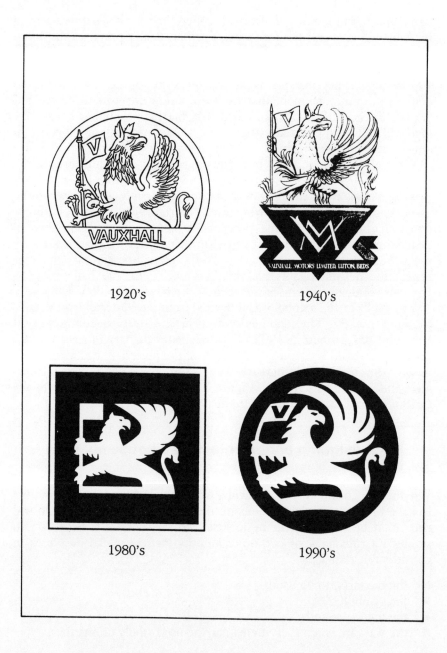

1920's

1940's

1980's

1990's

Figure 7.2 *The evolution of Vauxhall's trademark from the 1920s. The new logo for the 1990s symbolizes the new style of vauxhall, based on solid success*

how the 'HONDA' symbol and logotype may be used. The summary of the book explains that the 'basic system' specifies the fundamental rules applying to the shapes, usage, combinations and colours of the basic elements in the Honda Corporate Image & Design Development system.

The basic elements described in the book are:

- corporate logotype;
- Honda Automobile Division trademark ('H' mark);
- combination mark ('H' mark with corporate logotype) — see Figure 7.3;
- corporate image colours.

Figure 7.3 *The Honda logotype*

It is then emphasized that:

these basic elements are the most important factors in forming Honda's image and are the cornerstone of every form of customer communication or approach. Displaying the correct Honda image to the customer and having the customer recognize it as Honda's is important for two reasons:

1. it is the first step in promoting trust and assurance in the company, and correct appraisal of its products; and
2. it is a must if customers are to understand Honda's thinking and appreciate Honda's position as a corporation. For these reasons, usage of the basic elements must be in strict accordance with the rules given in the manual.

The book goes on to illustrate all the different ways in which the logo and logotype can be used, with strict attention to dimensions and relativity. The book includes a large number of examples of incorrect and banned usages of the corporate identity.

All major examples of new or revised corporate identity programmes will include a manual designed to see that the image is presented correctly.

The ICI corporate identity story

The new ICI logo (see Figure 7.1) which was announced in 1991 is another example of a logo developing by evolution. The familiar roundel started as a logo for Nobel and was adopted by ICI In 1969. The recent adaptation emphasizes the wording and the waves effect but the evolution from the original logo is quite clear.

Department for enterprise

When the Department of Trade and Industry decided to adopt a new house style to signal its policy of drawing together the many different operations of the new department, it opted for an innovative design using lower case letters which is certainly memorable if not particularly pleasing to the eye (see Figure 7.4).

the department for Enterprise

Figure 7.4 *A modern logo example of an old-fashioned style*

The BP story

The new corporate identity of BP in 1990 was reported to have cost £1 million. The company explained that this large sum covered an extensive research programme in Britain, the USA, the Far East, Australia and Germany. The new BP shield is the latest version of a logo that has remained much the same since it was introduced in 1920 — the result of a competition among employees.

Behind the decision to adopt a new identity lay an intensive study which examined the very nature of the BP Group and what its image had become. The devolution of the group into separate businesses, and a stream of acquisitions, had brought profound changes in its structure. Mr Russell Seal, Managing Director and Chief Executive Officer of BP Oil, said that every day BP talks to many audiences, the general public, governments, the media, financial institutions and all sorts of special interest groups. The new mark and visual style will enable BP, from corporate level right to the point of sale, to convey the same distinctive and coherent message.

Mr Hugh Norton, Managing Director and Chief Executive Officer of BP Exploration, stated that BP Exploration is able to operate around the world largely because communities, partners and governments recognize and esteem our achievements and our technical and commercial qualities. The shield logo represents and reinforces that reputation. It gives us recognition, access and credibility. Moreover, our universal use of the name BP Exploration, coupled with the new shield, will be a source of pride and unity amongst our geographically scattered employees.

A very visual umbrella

One of the most effective examples of a new visual identity is the Legal and General umbrella. Mr Tom Banks, Corporate Communications Manager of Legal and General Insurance Company, stated that 'when we started our relationship with Sampson-Tyrrell, our vision was to strengthen the image of our company. Today, independent research shows that we are now recognized as one of the best known and strongest insurance companies in Britain'.

The umbrella has been a great success because its use has been carefully monitored and it has been possible to exploit the umbrella creatively on television and other media.

The story of 'Prudence'

The Prudential Corporation plc decided it needed a new corporate identity programme as research had shown its image to be old-fashioned, staid and lumbering. The objective was to bring together all the companies within the group under a common banner and in a way which was appropriate to the Prudential's development as a major financial service provider, not just an insurance company.

Figure 7.5 *The new logo of the Prudential Corporation featuring 'Prudence'*

David Vevers, director of public affairs at Prudential, working with design consultants Wally Olins, considered many options but finally selected 'Prudence' which had appeared on the top of the Prudential's coat of arms since the company began in 1848 (see Figure 7.5). So the new identity, which included a distinctive and lively typeface, combined the company's traditional strengths with the new dynamism.

Barnardos

Dr Barnardos decided it was time to update their image by the adoption of a new name and a revised corporate identity. The changes were intended to support a dramatic restatement of the real Barnardos mission which could:

1. invigorate fundraising efforts and remotivate volunteers:
2. reforge links with those wanting to find better ways to help children in their own communities;
3. remove all stigma of being helped by Barnardos;
4. create a platform from which the charity could begin campaigning for improved laws and services for young people with special needs.

The new logo is shown in Figure 7.6.

Figure 7.6 *The new Barnardos logo*

Milner Gray's contribution to corporate identity

For many decades Milner Gray, CBE, RDI, PPCSD, AGI, senior partner of Design Research Unit, was the first choice of organizations wishing to adopt new corporate identities. The illustration (Figure 7.7), which is reproduced here with Milner Gray's permission, shows some of the different signs and symbols designed by him, most of which formed a part of wider design commissions for many different companies and organizations. It is interesting to notice how different these examples are although they were all acclaimed as highly successful by their respective owners.

In this chapter, I have quoted extensively, by permission, from a paper written by Milner Gray for his staff and students.

Mark for CEGB	*Royal Arms for Design Council*	*SS Oriana Ships Badge*
Mark for SIAD	*Balmoral Rangers Badge*	*Mark for Arts Club*
Building Centre Symbol	*Mark for Austin Reed*	*House Symbol for De La Rue*
Symbol for Pyrex Glass	*Trademark for Allen & Hanbury*	*Courage Trademark*

Figure 7.7 *A selection of signs and symbols designed by Milner Gray, most of which formed part of wider design commissions*

Summary

The different factors involved in corporate identity are depicted diagrammatically in Figure 7.8. Corporate design usually reflects contemporary ideas of acceptable art. However, some companies deliberately choose an old-fashioned style in an attempt to achieve memorability. The dti logo probably comes within this category. Few companies, however, are likely to wish to revert to old styles such as the logo of the Buffalo-San Diego Railroad Corporation, Figure 7.9.

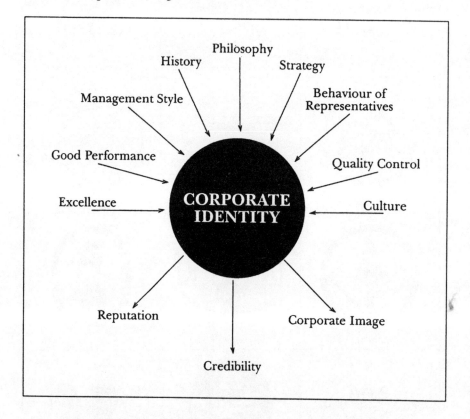

Figure 7.8 *The different factors involved in corporate identity*

Visual identity is too important to be left entirely to designers; senior management must be involved as it is such an important part of corporate policy. The public relations adviser will usually bring all the interested parties together so that the brief given to the designer can be as comprehensive as possible, but giving full scope for creativity and imagination.

Figure 7.9 *An early twentieth century design*

8

Community relations and corporate social responsibility

The concepts of community relations and corporate social responsibility have become enlarged by the increasing attention devoted to green issues and concern for the environment. These concerns are the responsibility of management but it is likely and desirable that the lead will be taken by public relations.

Protecting the environment

The Mexican Statement quoted in Chapter 1 emphasizes that public relations practice includes identifying trends and predicting their consequences. The current concern with environmental issues should have been foreseen as the subject was a live issue as long ago as 1970 — which was European Conservation Year.

The Institute of Public Relations identified conservation as deserving of careful consideration and invited Angus Maude, MP to discuss the subject in detail in his keynote address to the 1970 Annual Conference of the Institute. Despite that year being singled out as European Conservation Year, the attention given to protection of the environment was not very comprehensive at that time. In his address, Angus Maude said that technology can destroy but it can also solve its own problems if the will and incentive are there. His comments were prophetic and are worth quoting as they indicated so clearly how concern with the environment would become high on national and international agenda.

> Conservation is still largely a matter of economic policies and priorities. Whether our environment is spoiled, whether our air, water and soil are dangerously polluted, depends in the last resort on decisions which have to do with money — sometimes in the form of Government expenditure, sometimes of industrial profits.
>
> Government agricultural policy may determine the shape and appearance of the countryside: whether rolling hill country is maintained in its present form by grazing sheep, or reverts to

primeval scrub or has rows of Forestry Commission conifers planted on it. Too low a price for fat lambs, or the wrong policy for beef, can turn familiar fields into hedgeless prairies devoted to barley monoculture and in some places potential dust bowls.

The level of fuel oil duty may determine whether a power station is built inland, within easy rail journey of a coalfield, within pipeline distance of a port, or on the coast to work by nuclear energy.

The Government's allocation of money for roads may determine whether a motorway takes the easy course that destroys a valley or wrecks the line of a scarp, or takes the most costly but less destructive route.

Another crucial question is the extent to which Governments are prepared to interfere with profitable enterprise in the interests of the community as a whole. The community is beginning to say clearly that it is prepared to pay a price for the avoidance of pollution, noise and ugliness. The politician's job is to estimate how high a price is tolerable.

Protection of the environment is, of course, the joint responsibility of governments, companies and individuals. An example of how new scientific discoveries can seriously affect a company's operations was the announcement that CFC gas, as used in refrigeration and aerosols, was harming the ozone layer. This presented a very serious problem for Imperial Chemical Industries, the leading manufacturer in Britain of CFC gas. The company tackled the situation by starting an immediate research programme, costing £50 million, to find a suitable non-toxic substitute.

The public relations task was to explain the situation to the public and to publicize the reasons why it would take some time to phase out their use. Had the company taken the easy way out and simply closed down all its CFC-producing plants, there would have been very serious harm done to all the industries and hospitals relying on refrigeration. While urgently seeking replacement techniques and explaining the situation, ICI took a leading role in calling for a strengthening of the Montreal Protocol to include total phase-out of CFCs.

ICI Paints, which is a very large division of ICI, has taken the initiative in sponsoring the world's first academic symposium to investigate and discuss the potential risks to human health and the environmental impact of paints on the planet. This event was held in Singapore and was attended by experts from many countries. The full proceedings will be published and there will be a continuing dialogue to help further the understanding of the health and environmental aspects of paint.

The International Public Relations Association (IPRA) adopted a Code for Communication on Environment and Development at Nairobi in November 1991. The code is issued as a guide to members of the association for areas of practice related to the environment. It has nine clauses:

1. IPRA members accept that they have a responsibility to ensure that the information and counsel which they provide, and products or services which they promote, fall within the context of sustainable development.
2. Members shall endeavour to encourage their organizations, companies or clients to adopt policies which recognize that careless use of resources and disregard for the environment can lead to severe limitations for economic growth, grave social disruption and serious health hazards.
3. Members shall, where appropriate, counsel their companies, clients or organizations to undertake regular environmental assessments of products and operations and to produce and communicate environmental codes of practice or guidelines for their employees and other publics.
4. Members shall not publicize or promote products, organizations or services as having environmental benefit unless these benefits are demonstrable in the light of current science and knowledge.
5. Members shall endeavour at all times to promote openness and dialogue which fairly handle both facts and concerns related to the environment and development.
6. Members shall not seek to raise or respond to unrealistic environmental expectations but shall generally support organizations, products or services which are provably taking steps to improve environmental performance in a time scale which takes account of community concerns and government requirements as well as technological and economic constraints.
7. Members shall seek to develop programmes which counsel and communicate on the benefit of a balanced consideration of environmental, economic and social development factors.
8. Members shall provide a free flow of information within and through IPRA concerning environmental and development issues on an international level.
9. Members should be familiar with, and encourage the organizations they work for to support, and abide by, codes of practice of other internationally recognized organizations such as the United Nations and the International Chamber of Commerce.

Community relations

It is now generally accepted that a large company has a responsibility to the community in which it operates. Its first duty is to be efficient and profitable so that it can reward its shareholders and provide secure and well paid employment. It is equally important that the company should be a 'good citizen' and 'social leader'. These concepts of social responsibility developed first in the US but are now firmly established in Britain and other developed countries. The Confederation of British Industry published a report on this subject in 1973 and the Institute of Directors published a similar report in the same year.

Tom Frost, chief executive of National Westminster Bank plc, emphasized his company's concern with corporate social responsiblity in a recent speech. He said that in the decade ahead, as people become better informed, more articulate and more discerning, the expectations of corporate legitimacy — of the company benefiting society — is asserting itself. As stakeholders of all types place increasing emphasis on factors other than price, salary and dividends, the social responsibility record of a company will become more vital to its competitiveness.

Lord Laing of Dunphail, when chairman of United Biscuits, initiated the 'Percentage Club' to which many British companies belong. Member companies pledge to donate to the community one per cent of profits before tax.

Helping the community is not altruism but rather enlightened self-interest, but it is the community at large which benefits. There are obvious benefits to a company which can operate in a friendly community. Corporate social responsibility (CSR) usually includes the following elements:

- **Enterprise**: helping local entrepreneurs and supporting enterprise.
- **Education**: promoting new initiatives for young people.
- **Arts and culture**: assisting a wide range of artistic activities.
- **Environment**: supporting all local efforts to safeguard the quality of life.

Companies in the Percentage Club second members of their staff to help worthy causes. The men and women selected to be seconded are usually young executives in mid-term career or senior executives in their pre-retirement years.

Another well established service to the community is 'help in kind'. This assistance takes different forms according to the company's major activities. Some companies donate office or workshop accommodation, or materials like paint or timber, or redundant computers and other office equipment. (See case history of ICI Paints later in this chapter.)

CSR differs from sponsorship as the company does not seek any publicity or undue identification.

Many companies encourage suitable employees to take an active part in local government and local charities and societies. Encouragement usually includes giving the employees concerned reasonable time off when required.

It is quite usual for large organizations to hold an open day once or twice a year when families and friends can visit the works or headquarters and see for themselves what goes on. This promotes pride in the company, helps mutual understanding and assists recruitment and retention of employees.

The opportunities for spending time and resources on corporate social responsibility are almost infinite so it is necessary for each organization to take a cool, hard look at its programme in this field. Few people expect the business sector to operate as philanthropists, but accept that they will act in a spirit of enlightened self-interest. Free enterprise survives only by permission of society; it is not an inalienable right bestowed upon corporate executives and shareholders.

A clear view of what is responsible conduct, accompanied by actions and communication, is in the self-interest of both business and society. The following principles might be a good guide for companies considering their policy in this respect:

1. Select problems that rank high in local or national concern.
2. Concentrate efforts on a few areas where their impact and visibility are likely to be high.
3. Utilize effective marketing skills in communicating and publicizing your company's social and community programmes and their successes.
4. Minimize, or avoid completely, single interest corporate objectives that the public may see as self-serving.

Case history 9
Bringing new jobs to the North at Fort Sterling

Lancashire tissue paper manufacturer, Fort Sterling wished to undertake an investment programme which would double capacity at Ramsbottom in East Lancashire and ensure the company's competitive edge in the years ahead. They wished to plan an efficient construction programme which would minimize inconvenience and upset to the local community. Their proposal to invest £70 million on a major expansion programme creating up to 400 new jobs was wonderful news for the region, but the likely impact on local residents during the two-year construction period was of major concern.

Fort Sterling's paper mill, where the construction would take place, is in Ramsbottom, a traditional old mill town. Tight-knit terraces of stone run right up to the mill walls, and local residents feared an immediate future of heavy construction work, scores of lorries on narrow local roads, up to 500 construction workers descending on the small town, mud on the road during dirty winter weather, noisy pile driving, destruction of trees on the new site and general disruption to the town.

Faced with this dilemma, the American-owned company decided to seek public relations advice and help and engaged Rex Stewart Grayling North (RSGN) a Manchester based public relations consultancy. The brief was to devise a public relations strategy to establish effective communication between Fort Sterling and local residents, community leaders and the media. It was necessary to emphasize the positive benefits of the project while ensuring damage limitation. If the residents could feel that their interests were being taken into consideration at every step, and the demands of the local planning and environmental authorities could be satisfied, it was likely that construction could proceed according to schedule.

RGSN tackled this difficult assignment by researching the project from its planning stages and assessing opposition and support at the various stages of the project. The team assigned to the task included an account director with experience in the paper trade and an executive who had herself worked for some of the local papers.

Planning the strategy
Fort Sterling had already made major efforts to be a good neighbour. Residents were able to buy the company's tissue products at factory discount prices and a team of street cleaners was employed to keep local streets clear of waste paper. Meetings with residents had been held prior to the planning application, but communication had broken down and some residents had formed a local action group.

RSGN's priority was to build on those early contacts and to bring the residents again into communication with the company. The plan included reviving regular residents' committee meetings and suggesting setting up a 'hot line' whereby residents could telephone somebody at the mill whenever they had a question or a concern. Briefing packs were produced to provide comprehensive and accurate information to all interested parties. A notice-board was set up in a prominent position to keep the community up to date with developments, a regular residents newsletter was produced and briefing meetings were held with the two local MPs.

Besides the above initiatives, close contact was maintained with the contractors and consultants in order to be able to publicize 'good news' regarding locally placed orders, new local jobs and other positive stories. The Department of Trade and Industry had committed a £2 million grant towards the project, and Secretary of State Peter Lilley visited the construction site. This provided very good media coverage.

Evaluation
The success of the campaign was shown by the substantial reduction in the number of complaints from residents as they felt they were receiving consideration from the company. This was evidenced by analyzing the telephone calls which were being logged. Media comment on the project continued, on the whole, to be supportive. The company considered that the objective of regaining contact with the residents had been achieved.

A number of new projects have been established to strengthen the company's involvement with the local community. A nature reserve is being considered for an area of hilltop woodland on the Rossendale Mill site. A paper industry museum is a possibility. Local schools and colleges are being invited to take part in various projects.

Comment

This is a good example of an American company taking the advice of public relations consultants with a knowledge of local customs and susceptibilities.

Case history 10
A programme of Scottish national community
initiatives — BP Exploration

In April 1991, BP Exploration Operating Company Limited launched a series of Scottish national community initiatives under the title **BP Discovery Programme**. The series had four main themes:

1. Discover the environment.
2. Discover sport.
3. Discover commerce.
4. Discover the arts.

The programme is a major element of a wider spectrum of BP funded community schemes and projects in Scotland. The purpose of this particular scheme is to create opportunities for people, particularly the young and special needs groups, to discover their full potential. By extension, the programme reflects BP Exploration's commitment to becoming actively involved in the communities in which it lives and works.

Preparation and research

Early in 1990, a comprehensive community relations brief was drawn up by BP Exploration's Government and Public Affairs Department, setting out the main terms of reference for a community sponsorship programme. An independent feasibility study was commissioned in August 1990. Desk research confirmed the following trends in community-based sponsorship: sole sponsorship, concentration on a smaller number of sponsorships customized to the sponsor's requirements, and the use of research for evaluation.

Based on the initial research, the BP Discovery Programme was created, allowing BP the flexibility to tailor and modify community schemes to its geographic requirements.

Further independent market research was conducted among opinion formers and sponsorship users in the three months prior to the programme's launch. In-depth interviews were conducted with senior respondents from the education and public sectors, as well as environmental organizations, chambers of commerce, trade unions and secondary school teachers.

The results of this study confirmed that the community led nature of the proposed programme would meet their expectations.

Planning

The principal objectives of the BP Discovery Programme were agreed as follows:

- to build BP Exploration's profile as a good corporate citizen;
- to communicate their commitment to the communities in which they operate;
- to create the best possible return on sponsorship investment.

The planning stage covered five activities, conducted in parallel:

- to identify suitable components of the programme;
- to liaise with sponsored organizations to formulate strategy;
- to prepare fully itemized budgets;
- to create a corporate identity for the BP Discovery Programme and its principal schemes;
- to plan the launch arrangements.

Discover the environment

BP made contact with Scotland's largest youth organization, Youth Clubs Scotland and jointly created the *BP Grizzly Challenge*, a scheme inviting 1000 youth clubs all over Scotland to make a practical improvement to their local environment.

Discover sport

Scotland's only athletics awards scheme, the Thistle Awards, formed the major part of Discover Sport, with a new emphasis on special needs athletes being brought into the scheme by BP.

Discover commerce

BP became Scotland's largest supporter of Understanding Industry, the industry-in-education body.

Discover the arts

This comprised two separate sponsorships:

1. **Opening Acts**, one of Scotland's most successful theatre-in-education groups.
2. **The Arts is Magic**, Scotland's largest free integrated arts festival.

The budget

A fully itemized budget was prepared covering all the items involved in the sponsorship programme.

The corporate identity

Distinctive logos were devised for each part of the programme as well as for the BP Grizzly Challenge and the BP Thistle Awards.

Implementation

The BP Discovery Programme was launched by Magnus Magnusson at a special event attended by opinion formers and community representatives. A special photocall featured models dressed as wildlife, an athlete, a businesswoman and a harlequin, each representing the key elements in the scheme. Extensive picture coverage was achieved.

The BP Grizzly Challenge

This scheme was launched in April 1991 to all the affiliated youth clubs — 1000 in total — in Scotland. It is a challenge to young people to use their energy, ideas and teamwork to improve their local environment.

The first BP Grizzly Challenge attracted entries from 40 teams (165 young people) from all over Scotland. Chasing the top prize of a trip to the USA, 15 selected teams took part in a week-long residential course incorporating team building and environmental exercises as they prepared for the next stage — carrying out their projects.

Having completed their nine week projects, the teams qualified for the final stage, giving a presentation to the judging panel, HRH Princess Margaret and assembled guests. The resulting media coverage promoted both Youth Clubs Scotland and BP, and helped teams to attract support in their own communities.

The BP Thistle Awards

Disabled athletes and those with learning difficulties or mental handicap were included in the scheme. The main track and field events were launched at Edinburgh Meadowbank Sports Centre on 9 May 1991. A joint awards ceremony for the top schools and athletes taking part in the BP Thistle Awards was held for the first time at Meadowbank on 29 November 1991.

Discover Commerce

As part of this programme, BP Exploration is sponsoring 25 courses for Understanding Industry (UI), an educational trust which provides short courses for schools, covering all aspects of business and commerce, taught by industry volunteers, including representatives from BP. BP's sponsorship allowed UI to recruit extra staff and to increase its activities in Scottish schools, and to improve its briefing materials.

For the 1992 school summer term, a business challenge was introduced. This involved the creation of business plans for fictitious start-up companies.

Discover the Arts

With BP's support, the Opening Arts Theatre Company toured round 24 secondary schools throughout Scotland with a production of Steinbeck's *Of mice and men*. Continuing support from BP has helped the company to secure greater support from The Scottish Arts Council.

BP Exploration is one of the major sponsors of *Arts is Magic*, Scotland's largest free integrated arts festival, and will sponsor the event in 1992 for the third successive year. In addition to financial support, BP provides considerable help in kind and sits on the festival's management board.

Evaluation of the programme

The strategy for measuring the results of this extensive programme was as follows:

1. market research;
2. qualitative and quantitative analysis of media coverage;
3. informal feedback from opinion formers, employees and scheme participants;
4. written reports from sponsored organizations.

BP Discovery Programme has been a tremendous success and the established format will be repeated in future years. A notable yardstick was media coverage in the month of October 1991 alone, which exceeded all editorial coverage on community projects for the whole BP Group in Scotland in 1990. Measurement of the BP Discovery Programme is now a part of BP Group's regular attitude surveys, which cover a wide range of issues and target audiences.

To increase the sophistication of measurement of the BP Discovery Programme, from February 1992, media coverage is being analyzed using the highly advanced evaluation computer package. This provides reports on the size of the article or photograph, its position on the page, the frequency of publication and other relevant factors.

Comment

This case history is a good example of an integrated community relations programme which has been carried out with imagination and enthusiasm on a grand scale and has reaped the deserved benefits of such a comprehensive programme.

Case history 11
Painting the community — Dulux

The 'Dulux Community Projects Scheme' has been operating since 1980. It has achieved its purpose of bringing ICI Paints into direct contact with many sections of the community and has given the company a human face while maintaining its position as the brand leader in paint. The scheme has been promoted entirely by public relations without any advertising support.

Research

In the late 1970s, ICI Paints became concerned that their image among customers was becoming too 'high tech'. Research in the UK undertaken to establish the public's attitude to ICI Paints' Dulux brand showed that while consumers credited ICI with making the best paint, they regarded Dulux as being removed from everyday life. 'Aloof' and 'too scientific' were the adjectives most commonly used when describing the brand. Dulux conjured up visions of men in white coats and laboratories where correct formulae were produced. The brand did not convey the warmth, approachability and friendliness which ICI felt was essential if they were to be able to encourage the use of Dulux in the home.

In view of these research findings, it was considered essential to make consumers more comfortable with the Dulux brand. This had to be achieved, however, without losing the positive aspects of being brand leader in the UK retail paint sector and widely perceived as the very best quality paint.

A public relations consultancy, Welbeck Golin/Harris, was briefed to devise a campaign which would change consumer attitudes towards the Dulux brand. The stated objectives were:

- to create a programme which would clearly associate Dulux with caring, warmth, friendliness and approachability;
- to continue to associate the brand with the technical excellence of ICI Paints, but to offer this as a means of reassurance rather than intimidation;
- to underline the brand's position as the brand leader;
- to make direct contact with consumers as well as via the media.

Planning

In planning the campaign, it was decided that it was necessary to create a public relations programme which would reflect the new brand values and be of social significance in line with ICI's responsibility as the brand leader. It was agreed that the activity should operate at grassroots level, involving all sectors of the community so that its media appeal would reach the broad spectrum of current and potential paint users. Moreover, the effect of the programme would be long term and the altered public perception of the brand would be sustained.

The programme which was developed to meet the demands of the brief, was the **Dulux Community Projects Awards Scheme**, which was launched in 1980 and is still continuing to meet ICI's objectives by emphasizing the company's commitment to the community, and has helped to change public attitude towards the brand. The concept was for ICI Paints to create a scheme whereby they would donate large quantities of Dulux paint to suitable voluntary groups and charities throughout the United Kingdom. Any group could apply, providing the work they planned using the paint would benefit the community.

The country was divided into five regions and an independent panel of judges, drawn from the voluntary sector, was appointed. This scheme ensured that media coverage would be generated throughout the country and that Dulux would be portrayed as the generous patron of the scheme, rather than a manufacturer with a vested interest.

Implementation

The scheme was launched in Spring 1980 with a reception attended by national press, consumer interest magazines, radio and television, and London based news agencies who syndicated the story to regional publications. In addition, a direct mail campaign was undertaken to all UK based national charitable and voluntary organizations, inviting them to pass on the information to their regional members.

Posters and application forms were produced and distributed widely through libraries and Citizens Advice Bureaux, together with current Dulux colour cards. All successful applicants could choose any paint from the current Dulux retail range, rather than be forced to accept old or discontinued lines.

Administration of the scheme is handled by Welbeck Golin/Harris who have a part of their offices devoted to The Dulux Community Projects Office. All applications are studied here and summarized before being passed to the independent panel of judges for assessment. Awards are made on an annual basis.

A special selection category has been added to the scheme. Those groups judged by the panel of judges to be most deserving because of the creativity of their project, and its value to the community, are given a special cash award. This generates further media coverage and provides good 'before' and 'after' photography.

Evaluation

The statistics illustrate the success of the scheme. On average, more than 10,000 charities and voluntary groups apply for free paint each year. During the twelve years of the programme, over 4,500 organizations have completed projects helped by the distribution of £500,000 worth of free paint. Media coverage continues annually in the national and regional press and in the radio and broadcast media.

The company considers that by regularly involving charities and voluntary groups, it is associating the brand with an image of caring, warmth and friendliness which has helped Dulux remain the brand leader. Qualitative research has confirmed this view.

Comment

This is one of the most successful and sustained examples of aiding community relations by donations in kind on a planned basis.

Case history 12
Encouraging child art in South Africa

This scheme has been operated by the large insurance company Santam for 30 years. The project has three main branches: child art, bursaries for school leavers and bursaries for art students. The company has acted in the firm belief that commerce and industry must make a positive contribution to the cultural, educational and moral welfare of the entire Southern African community.

Santam launched its first child art project in 1963. The purpose of the original project was:

- to encourage an appreciation of art among the youth;
- to create in the minds of the youth a sense of trust in the future of South Africa;
- to allow children of all races to share in a common project;
- to afford the company exposure at a level other than business.

It was never a competition as such and at the request of the education authorities, children are not given cash prizes. Monetary awards are only made to the schools or in the form of bursaries for further study. Over the years, care had to be taken that themes with a wide interest should be adopted so that all children, regardless of their race, culture or language could participate.

What had started as a purely child project, expanded to meet the demand for help for students to attend universities or technikons throughout South Africa. The bursaries are not limited to fine art or sculpture, but are also available to students of subjects such as dress designing, photography and graphic design. The scheme changes year by year to meet demand and there is continuing research to determine changing needs and to adjust the programme accordingly.

Planning of the child art project starts a year ahead with the selection of a theme. Santam always tries to choose themes which are educational, leaning towards environmental consciousness and which are in tune with national or international trends. For example, the theme chosen for 1991 was 'Our Precious Earth' which was seen as a contribution to international concern with the survival of our planet.

Invitations are sent out to thousands of schools and the theme is also publicized through the press. About 20,000 entries are usually received each year and the judges are normally art inspectors from various centres in South Africa. The entries are sorted into age groups and arrangements made to return unselected entries to the schools and art centres concerned. Students are invited to apply for bursaries and are required to submit a portfolio of their work by way of colour slides. One panel judges the work of the school leavers and another panel judges the work of the university and technikon students. The works of the bursary winners are collated for distribution to universities and technikons for viewing.

Apart from Santam's own travelling exhibition, other exhibitions are selected to meet special needs. Over the years, special educational projects have also been mounted — these include an art teacher's training project, a special graphic art project for schools and a full colour brochure of all the selected works.

The success of the scheme has increased year by year and Santam are satisfied that they have achieved all their objectives.

Comment

Insurance companies need public relations to give them reputation and credibility as confidence is the essential basis of their business. Santam chose wisely in deciding to concentrate on promoting art among the young as this could avoid any multi-racial problems. The fact that the project has been expanded regularly and has continued uninterrupted for 20 years is proof of Santam's wise choice of an avenue for their community relations.

Case history 13
Managing forests and vast nature reserves in Sweden

This is an account of the successful total communications programme carried out by the Swedish Domän Group from 1988 to 1991.

The Group had long played a key role in the management of Swedish forests and providing public facilities for outdoor life. About 20 per cent of the total area of Sweden, including considerable parts of the country's nature reserves, were administered by Domän with its 5500 employees and a turnover of £350 million. In the early 1980s, the reputation of Domän was fairly negative, partly due to widespread criticism of Swedish forestry methods. This was reflected by poor morale within the organization. A new director general and CEO was appointed, Mr Bo Hedstrom, and with the help of his new executive team, he decided to make a positive effort to restore Domän's reputation by systematic communication with key target groups and with the general public. A position of vice-president, public relations was created in 1986 with a seat in the Domän executive group.

In that new executive group, a series of decisions with long-range consequences for Domän were taken, including a reorganization with reduced staff at headquarters and with more responsibility being left to the forestry districts. Of great significance to the public relations function were the decisions to:

1. ban the use of herbicides (in 1986);
2. change towards a more ecologically-oriented forestry, including the training of 1000 foresters in a special programme called 'Our forests are threatened';
3. make a strong commitment to environmental and opinion-building activities.

Public relations planning was integrated into the total budget and planning process of Domän, and a dialogue on public relations issues started with all resource unit members of the Group.

The starting point
Opinion polls in 1988 showed that Swedish forestry management was quite unpopular and misunderstood. Only 20 per cent of Swedes knew that the annual increase in Swedish forests was greater than the volume felled. Nearly half the population believed that the forests were sprayed with pesticides every year, although spraying with herbicides had been prohibited since 1986.

Public opinion expected and demanded Domän, as state owned, to be more environment conscious than the forest industries. The group was expected not only to produce and deliver the best possible raw material to the pulp and sawmill industries, but also to care about the multitude of wildlife, to safeguard wilderness areas, to provide good fishing and hunting possibilities, and at the same time to be more conscious of the environment than all its competitors — a very delicate balancing act.

A communications platform
A 'communications platform' was agreed upon by the Domän executive group, including the following key elements:

- The management philosophy shall permeate all information work.
- Devotion and understanding by all employees of the aims and direction of the Group is one of the most important conditions for success.
- The managers shall seize every opportunity for encouragement, but, with their staffs, find out the reasons for any failure to reach the Group's objectives and draw the correct conclusions.
- Internal discussion and debate is an important prerequisite to making the right decisions and for the staff to feel at ease and to enjoy job satisfaction.
- We should benefit from the advantages of size but act towards individuals and organizations in such a way that they do not feel they are running against a colossus. Whenever necessary, we shall admit to shortcomings in our work in an open manner.

Planning
It was agreed that the public relations policy to be adopted could be summed up as:

> The Domän group combines demands for profitability with strict environmental control and an active contribution to outdoor life — the so-called 'Multiple use concept'. Initial concentration would be on communicating with both employees and the general public. This policy was enshrined in a three year plan, 1988–1990, 'The communication platform and the verbal identity'.

In order to help managers at all levels in their communication work a document was produced: 'The public relations tools — aids to information and public relations work within the Domän group'. This document was essentially a do-it-yourself public relations handbook for beginners, with step by step advice on everything from oral communication with forestry workers to tips on media relations. A series of seminars for 400 line managers helped to implement positive public relations thinking throughout the organization.

New life was breathed into the company's house journal *Domänposten* and the contents changed from light reading and gossip to concentration on results, working methods and prospects.

Pilot projects for communication with a few local committees were tested, with a view to a wider implementation at a later date. Such efforts were, of course, dependent on the degree to which regional and local managers were prepared to accept public relations as a vital part of their responsibilities and as a strategic management instrument, in competition with other time-consuming managerial tasks.

These managers had a good story to tell their publics. In tune with changing public opinion, Swedish forestry had committed itself to combating acid rain and air pollution problems. One thousand foresters had been trained by university teams to adopt a more ecology-conscious programme. Domän maintained 1500 fishing waters and 40 non-commercial areas open to the public.

Information policy

The new Communication Handbook emphasized that internal information should have top priority. All employees directly affected by events or changes, within or outside Domän, should be informed about these and their positive or negative consequences. Active contacts with authorities, politicians, institutions, schools and other target groups should be established and developed with a view to exerting influence on working conditions.

All recreation areas and public areas were used as information centres to spread information about Domän and its positive policy of promptness, sincerity and coordination. Regular contact with the public is secured through its annual wall calendar: *Nature och Fritid* (Nature and Leisure). This calendar includes selected facts about Domän and encourages readers to contact *DomänTurist* about the choice of leisure time activities offered by Domän. Above all, however, the calendar offers 12 exquisite photographs of Swedish nature during the four seasons of the year. The circulation of the calendar is 2.2 million to a total Swedish population of 8.5 million. A Gallup poll in 1990 showed that as many as 700,000 calendars were hanging on the walls of offices and homes.

The best selling publications of Domän, however, are its leisure time folders. About 40 non-commercial recreation areas are presented in separate A6 size folders with maps, basic facts about sites of special interest and brief information about Domän. Several million copies of these folders are distributed each year, mainly through the state and municipal tourist offices.

Fishing in the Domän waters is available for anyone who pays a small licence fee. To encourage and inform fishing enthusiasts, the quarterly Domänfiske (Doman Fishing) is produced by the group, and about 70 000 Swedes renew their fishing licences annually and get information on fish, fishing and Domän through this magazine.

Information for schools and students is prepared by the Domän public relations department dealing with such subjects as: *Our forest; The Seedling; The Tree.*

Evaluation

At the end of the three year programme, 1988–1992, some basic results of the work could be measured and evaluated.

1. Compared with the leading forest industries, Domän had left its bottom ranking and had achieved the top position with regard to both knowledge and attitude.
2. Out of 8.5 million inhabitants in Sweden, probably 50 per cent were reached by the magazine *Nature and Leisure*, and 700,000 calendars are displayed on the wall.

3. Domän registered over 25 million day-visits per year to its recreation areas.
4. Through the Domän catalogue, 575,000 nights were booked in the Domän holiday cottages.
5. 70,000 fishing enthusiasts registered and purchased fishing licences for the Domän lakes and waters.
6. The house journal received very favourable marks in externally conducted reader polls despite, or thanks to, the new editorial policy of including more business news. The journal won first prize for its front cover in a competition among all Swedish house journals.

Tailpiece

On 1 July 1992, the whole picture changed with the reorganization which turned Domän into a limited company, prior to later flotation on the Stock Exchange. This change of company structure means that in many respects the public relations of the group will have to be restarted. The success achieved during 1988–92, on an annual budget of £2 million, with a staff of six will, however, form an excellent model for the partly new company to follow.

(This case history is a summary of the full case study which received a golden award in the 1990 IPRA Golden World Awards for Excellence. Our thanks to Lars-Olle Larsson who, as senior vice-president, public relations for Domän during the period discussed, was in charge of the planning and implementation. He is now senior vice-president, public relations of Sweden Post.)

Comment

This case history is included in the chapter dealing with the environment since the activities of Domän are directly related to the way a country deals with its ecological and environmental problems and opportunities. It could equally well have been included in the chapter on corporate relations since it illustrates the positive part played by the public relations policy in the restructuring of the organization.

Case history 14
IMPACT India in action

In November 1981, a seminar at Leeds Castle, England brought together an international group of scientists, health specialists and politicians of world standing under the chairmanship of Lord Home. The meeting finished with the adoption of the Leeds Castle Declaration: 'Avoidable disability is a prime cause of economic waste and human deprivation in all countries, indus- trialized and developing. This loss can be reduced rapidly'.

In order to translate the recommendations into action. IMPACT was created. It represents a unique initiative by bringing together the resources of the United Nations with the vigour of private enterprise and the expertise of governments with the dedication of community self-help.

The global launch of IMPACT in India

India was chosen to be the site of the global launch of the IMPACT initiative because it had the capacity to tackle disability prevention and had developed a number of low-cost technologies useful in preventing disabilities. The major thrust of the IMPACT India initiative was to be on the level of primary health care: prevention of diseases like poliomyelitis, goitre, blindness and serious infections. About two million people become disabled in India each year.

The success achieved by IMPACT India in Madras, Bombay and elsewhere was the result of coordinating available resources in the public and private sectors into a working whole. Without this, the various inputs would have remained disjointed and isolated. For example, Voltas Limited, India's largest marketing, engineering and manufacturing enterprise, has donated the skills of its senior management, communications and technical professionals to firmly establish IMPACT in India. IMPACT acts as a catalyst, using the strengths of the business houses to work with the Government on mass welfare programmes. The project is considered to be an excellent model for the entire developing world.

IMPACT India's role was:

- communicating with agencies, both governmental and non-governmental, to secure resources;
- communicating with the Government to get sanctions and support;
- communicating awareness in the beneficiaries in order to create demand.

Folk media is popular in India. It has been a form of public communication through the ages and continues to be one of the most important media for development and social change. For example, IMPACT India used this effectively to communicate the need for immunization. Through street plays and puppetry, the message of immunization was taken into the streets and community centres. College students and volunteers performed street plays with a health education theme which reinforced opinions that made immunization socially acceptable.

The influence and contribution of IMPACT India

IMPACT India has used communication to harness existing resources and has exerted a salutary influence on established agencies and organizations. As a government and UN promoted initiative backed by prominent leaders of the Indian business community, it has lent legitimacy to its developmental objectives and to the people and organizations involved. Communication has been the basis of success. IMPACT India is an inspiration to action, a call to identify talent and to harness it in the best interests of the community.

The director of IMPACT India is Mrs Zelma Lazarus, general manager of corporate relations at Voltas Limited. Previously she had been 'loaned' by the company to act as regional consultant to United Nations development programmes. The willingness by Voltas Limited to second Mrs Lazarus for this vital development work is an excellent example of community relations.

Comment
This involvement of a leading Indian public relations practitioner in development projects of such national importance is quite appropriate as the techniques and strategies involved are similar to those required for success in typical public relations programmes. What is more remarkable perhaps is the willingness of a major Indian company to second a senior executive to this work on a long-term commitment.

A detailed case study of the work of IMPACT India during its first years of operation was published by Simone St Anne in January 1992 as part of her degree requirements at Cornell University.

9
Research, measurement and evaluation

Since public relations is an integral part of management, a measure of its success is the profitability, or otherwise, of the whole organization, but if one considers the use of public relations in organizing or supporting a special event it may be possible to obtain a direct measurement.

It is understandable that companies, and particularly their accountants, want to know what they are getting for their money in every department. The main difficulty in measuring public relations activity is in isolating its effects from other events and circumstances. If the objectives have been carefully researched, discussed in detail and approved by the Board, they will provide a benchmark against which success can be assessed. A comparison between what was expected and what was achieved gives an indication of how successful the programme has proved, but tells little as to whether the same or better results could have been achieved in other ways and possibly with less cost or allocation of resources.

Research is usually considered under two headings: *pure or basic research* and *applied research*. In public relations practice, basic research covers the type conducted by sociologists, psychologists and other social scientists who seek to discover how human beings communicate and interact. The results of these enquiries can provide valuable information and behavioural principles which are invaluable to public relations professionals in planning programmes for their managements or clients.

Applied research

The International Public Relations Association carried out a survey of the different kinds of applied research which play a useful part in practice. Seven broad areas were identified:

1. **Attitude or opinion research**: which is designed to find out how people feel or what they think about a particular institution, business or subject.
2. **Motivation research**: designed to find out what people think or how they act.

3. **Research to identify social or economic trends** that may affect a particular organization or its public relations programmes.
4. **Marketing research**: designed to find out what people buy or use, or what they would prefer or could be encouraged to buy.
5. **Copy research**: designed to find out whether certain communications will be read and understood.
6. **Readership research**: designed to find out whether people have received and retained information from advertising and other communications materials that have been published or disseminated.
7. **Evaluation research**: designed to measure the success or failure of particular public relations projects or programmes compared with their intended objectives.

Opinion research

Research can be of positive value in many aspects of public relations. Robert M Worcester, chairman of Market & Opinion Research International (MORI), stated in an article in the *IPRA Review* November 1983, that there are 30 different ways, under four main headings, in which research can be used advantageously in public relations practice. These groups are: qualitative testing of concepts, pre-campaign measures, monitoring a campaign, and the use of analysis.

Qualitative testing of the concept

Research can be employed to assess probable public reaction to new services. to examine the likely impact of a new corporate identity or any new plans which are likely to affect public opinion. Figure 9.1 lists the uses of primary research methods.

Pre-campaign measures

Many possibilities come under this heading:

- testing public reaction to proposals for privatization or other contentious issues such as Sunday trading;
- measuring support for issues like lead-free petrol or field sports;
- ascertaining willingness to support charities, and measuring perceptions — accurate and inaccurate — of their functions;
- assessing the image of a company and its products;
- measuring the perceived strengths of special interest groups:
- assessing reactions to proposed diversification;
- determining the most effective ways of communicating with special groups and how these groups would prefer to be communicated with;

Technique	Most appropriate uses
Surveys	Determination of target groups' attitudes and motivations; assessing relationships between target group characteristics and attitudes or behaviour; evaluation of awareness, and impact of campaigns;
Observation	Examination under natural conditions of peoples' reactions and behaviour in different situations and in response to various stimuli;
Experimentation	Evaluation of the cause-and-effect relationship between various factors involved in a situation;
Focus Groups	Exploratory investigation of problems to establish hypotheses or uncover factors to be tested in further research;
Panels/Omnibus	Where continuous measurement of changes in attitudes, opinions, or behaviour is required or for the tracking of campaigns;
Simulation	Where many complex interrelationships exist between factors which need to be tested for predictive purposes.

Figure 9.1 *Uses of primary data collection techniques*

- to investigate public attitudes to the need for new facilities such as airports;
- ascertaining public awareness — or lack of it — on relevant issues;
- Evaluating editors' personal attitudes on sensitive issues.

Monitoring a campaign

Surveys and opinion research among the general public can yield valuable clues to the impact and effect of public relations activities on behalf of companies, or industry associations or government departments. Similarly, it is possible to assess results of internal communication programmes or new types of staff training.

The use of analysis

As in advertising research, the juxtaposition of recall (*visibility*) with attitude shift (*real effect*) can be very revealing for judging the cost-effectiveness of a campaign.

Comparing 'exposed' and 'unexposed' groups in a pre-post measurement can yield reliable information about the effect of a public relations campaign as it eliminates the effect of extraneous factors.

MORI carries out regular omnibus surveys of adults' opinions in Great Britain on a wide range of subjects and it is possible to have your particular questions added to one of these surveys without undue cost. The results of the omnibus survey can be broken down to give information on different groups or sub-groups. For example, it is customary to talk about the City but it is often vital to distinguish between brokers and institutional investors. In addition, MORI conducts several annual surveys among a wide variety of audiences. These include both analysts and institutional investors, MPs, peers and a wide variety of journalists.

Simple readership analysis can help to determine media priorities, but further analysis can give greater refinement. It is possible to produce a 'criss-cross' analysis to show the degree of overlap between any two selected media. MORI regularly determine both the normal national daily and Sunday readership habits and also which media they consider to be of greatest value to them; also the readership and effect of their particular trade press. Other methods of media analysis are described in Chapter 5.

Opinion research, as carried out professionally by organizations like MORI, is only one of the research methods which can play a useful part in public relations practice.

Excellence in research

Professor Tim Traverse-Healy has criticized four types of research as falling short of characterizing excellence: simple reviews of output, informal research, research undertaken primarily to achieve publicity, and research aiming only at evaluation or justification.

There are other ethical issues in the field of research which may cause worry. These include deceptive practices, invasion of privacy and inconsistency in interviewing and evaluation.

An aid to scientific management

The most important use of research is as an aid to scientific management before, during and after the completion of public relations programmes. The following are examples of the correct use of research in this field:

- The number of messages sent and activities planned.
- The number of placements and activities.
- The degree of exposure or target involvement.
- The number who record the messages and attended the events.
- The number who have learnt the message.
- The number who have changed their opinions.
- The number who have changed their attitudes.
- The number who have behaved in the desired fashion.
- The number who have repeated this behaviour.
- The effect of the activity on the social and cultural environment.

Methods of evaluation

For many years Dr Walter Lindenmann has been advocating a more planned and scientific approach to public relations research. He has recently outlined a novel way of distinguishing between different levels of the measurement of the results of programmes.[*] He emphasizes the importance of setting specific goals and objectives at the outset against which the success of the programme can be evaluated.

Lindenmann distinguishes between 'outputs', 'outgrowths' and 'outcomes'. When press cuttings are measured and assessed it is a measure of output, without yielding any quantitative guide to results. To know if a public relations programme really has succeeded, it is necessary to consider outgrowths and outcomes.

Outgrowths are what happens or takes place after a public relations programme has been in operation for some time. When people do, or do not pay attention to the messages which are being disseminated, when they understand the arguments and retain and remember them, this can be evaluated as outgrowth measures.

When people change their attitudes or opinions because of the public relations activities that have taken place, and when they actually change their behaviour because of what has been happening, Lindenmann characterizes these results as **outcome** measures.

Outputs can be measured by literature searches and secondary analysis of data collected by others, the conducting of simple opinion polls, and the use of content analysis techniques to measure quantitatively what appears in the media.

Outgrowths can be measured by a mix of qualitative and quantitative data collection techniques, including such methodologies as the conducting of focus groups, depth interviews with opinion leader groups, and extensive polling of key target audience groups either by telephone, face-to-face interviews or by mail.

[*] European Hollis Directory 1992-3

Measuring outcomes requires more sophisticated methodologies, such as the conducting of before and after polls (pre- and post-tests), the development of experimental designs, the utilization of unobtrusive data collection methods such as observation, participation, and role playing, or the conducting of comprehensive, multifaceted communication audits.

This analysis by Dr Lindenmann is valuable in clarifying the possibilities of carrying out research at different levels of sophistication. When senior management calls for measurement of results from public relations activities they should be informed of the complexity and cost of really valid measurement and evaluation. There is no simple answer; an array of different tools and techniques are required to assess correctly the impact or 'outcome' of public relations.

Using research as association

A potentially powerful use of research is to enhance a company's reputation by identifying the organization with an important topic of public interest. When completed, the results are published with the sponsoring company's name prominently attached to it. An example was the BUPA sponsored seminars based on research into subjects such as stress and smoking.

Some final observations on public relations research

Typically, research in public relations serves three functions. Frequently, it may be used to confirm assumptions about the state of public opinion. This can provide a very useful back-up function, in many ways analogous to the use of quality control systems in manufacturing.

A second role of research is to clarify questions on which limited information is available or on which apparently contradictory data are to be found. Research can help to identify, for example, the difference between what people really mean when they say they like or dislike an organization — the reasons they cite for these feelings, and even the origin of these feelings.

Finally, research occasionally sheds light on obscure aspects of public relations problems. The actual process of defining the design and assigning priorities to areas of investigation often elicits valuable insight into the nature of the problem itself. (This final section is based on IPRA Gold Paper No 3 on Public Relations Research.)

10
Internal public relations

The modern expression 'human resource development' has replaced the former term 'industrial relations' and this recognizes the fact that the employees of a company are very valuable assets. So the need to protect this valuable resource reinforces the moral obligation to provide the best possible conditions for all concerned.

The ideal relationship between owners or managers and employees requires truthful and regular communication. The following seven conditions are important for harmony in the workplace:

1. Full and truthful information, flowing freely up, down and sideways.
2. Trust and confidence between employer and employees.
3. Healthy and safe working conditions.
4. Fair and equitable remuneration.
5. Continuity of work without conflict.
6. Work satisfaction, most of the time, for each employee.
7. Pride in the organization and optimism for its future.

In industrial relations, public relations will usually work closely with the personnel department to seek and retain a high quality and contented work force. Neglect of communication will encourage rumours and false ideas and allow distorted concepts to form and gain currency by default. The 'grapevine' flourishes in these circumstances.

Effective internal communication

Effective communication is particularly important at three stages of employment:

1. Initially, when recruitment advertising and interviews should be followed by orientation material and induction meetings to inform on company facilities, culture and traditions.
2. During the years of service, when all employees need regular information and job-related news. Announcements must be made in good time of special events and rewards such as bonuses, pensions, compensation and merit awards.

3.   At termination or interruption of work, whether caused by illness, reorganization, redundancy, dismissal or retirement.

At all these stages, good, clear communication is very important and should not be left to chance or the grapevine.

Internal communication must be planned and implemented systematically. This will avoid the six fundamental mistakes identified by Harvard Professor, Daniel Quinn Mills:

1.   Management dictates too much and listens too little.
2.   Too little of what is communicated is understood.
3.   Too much of the content is of concern to management but not to the workers.
4.   Too much propaganda is communicated.
5.   There is too little candour.
6.   Communication bears too little relation to the possibility of change.

A measure of the problem is that when employees are asked to list their best sources of information, current research reveals that the grapevine comes first, followed by their immediate supervisors, company publications and other media, with face-to-face meetings coming last. Since good communication will usually drive out bad communication, the answer to the grapevine menace is to step up effective ways of keeping the work force fully informed and in good time. No longer should workers leaving a factory find out from their evening newspaper that their works is being closed forthwith. There are well-documented reports of this having happened many times in Britain in the past.

It is important to remember that employees constitute both an external public and an internal one. Opinion about the company, based on bias or rumour, and voiced outside to family, friends and other contacts can have a very bad effect on reputation. If many of the workers complain about their treatment and working conditions, the company's reputation is bound to suffer. On the other hand, good vibrations will have a strong ripple effect and will communicate themselves quickly and effectively. As in all areas of public relations, good performance must always precede good reputation.

An internal communications programme should harmonize with the corporate culture of the organization which is created by the shared values of the employees and the organization. A communications programme that does this will promote greater job satisfaction among employees and elevate their status. It is a truism that every employee of a company should be a public relations spokesperson for the organisation and should wish to raise the company's profile and reputation.

Where there is continuity of employment, there is likely to be good relations with the community. It is difficult for a company to pursue an active policy of corporate social responsibility if the working conditions inside the concern are poor, resulting in rapid labour turnover.

The pursuit of excellence

The pursuit of excellence can be a very good target for internal public relations. Inspection is an important aspect of all types of manufacture or production and it is a pity that so often a defeatist attitude is adopted by management and transmitted to workers. To preach that 'rejects must be kept to a minimum' is defeatist. A more enlightened approach is to seek 100 per cent success. Monetary or other appropriate reward can be given to individuals or groups who achieve 100 per cent excellence.

Employee morale can be enhanced by the introduction of competitive awards between departments or sections, or between different branches of a large company. The awards can be given for safety, new ideas, good timekeeping, regularity of attendance, or output free from rejects. Where awards are given, they should be valuable enough to match expectations. If new ideas make a considerable contribution to production methods, or the saving of time or money, the awards should be correspondingly generous.

Methods of internal communication

There are official channels for communication with employees, such as joint consultative machinery and through the unions. New techniques of consultation have been introduced, such as briefing groups in which small meetings of employees are held regularly for their managers to keep them up to date on new developments. Other opportunities for face-to-face communication are being tried.

These new ideas are very promising but there is a need to employ many different methods of keeping the work force informed and motivated. House journals are one of the well-established tools. They are still the most common method of imparting information regularly and the production and use of house journals has been discussed in Chapter 6. Two refinements of this have been employed successfully. Some companies with many different branches or factories have replaced their house journal with a regular video which is sent to every branch, where arrangements are made for employees to watch it in company time. One of the first organizations to use videos on a large scale was the Coca-Cola Corporation. Another pioneer in this field was GTE in Florida. Another method makes use of modern advances in information technology. AT & T has started using electronic mail to send a daily newspaper to employees (see case history 18 later in this chapter).

Notice boards, wall newspapers and bulletin boards

These methods of direct contact with employees can be effective, if placed strategically and carefully controlled. A responsible person should be in charge so that irrelevant or outdated material can be removed.

Case history 15
Building on strength — from Trusthouse Forte to Forte

The change of corporate name from Trusthouse Forte to Forte in 1992, and the rebranding, represented a significant communication challenge. If it was to be successful, it was vital that all Forte staff should have a clear understanding of the rationale for change and its implications and, when questioned, be able to explain it with conviction and enthusiasm to customers and suppliers alike.

The internal communications initiative constituted an integral part of the overall communications programme. It was researched, planned and implemented by an in-house team supported by external agencies.

Research
The first step was to set up a research programme to establish the staff's current attitudes towards Trusthouse Forte. The research was conducted in two phases: through the use of semi/structured interviews with managers and employees throughout the divisions, and by using a questionnaire to 2500 members of staff. The responses helped to determine the communication policy, the nature of the communication process and opportunities to improve the original ideas.

Planning
The results of the research indicated that the internal audiences fell into four categories. They were:

1. Board members and senior executives.
2. Senior and middle operational executives.
3. Unit and departmental managers.
4. Front line staff.

The research showed that staff would welcome close involvement with corporate decisions. In particular, it was widely felt among respondents that the programme should have a mechanism to enable staff to feed back their comments on the changes, leading to long-lasting improvements. These reactions were welcome, as it was desired to generate as much staff involvement as possible in the communication process to enhance their understanding of the rationale of the rebranding.

Key communicators
It was decided to develop a team of 450 'key communicators' drawn from senior and middle operational executives. They were spread throughout the

divisions and it was hoped they would play an important role as opinion formers. The main topics to be addressed were:

- new corporate name;
- rebranding of operations;
- restating of corporate values;
- rationale behind the change;
- role and responsibility of each individual and potential benefits.

Implementation

A critical constraint was the need for confidentiality prior to the posting of the annual report as shareholders had to approve the proposals at the AGM. The Cascade programme was therefore split into four phases, the first to coincide with the announcement of the proposal to shareholders and the others to be implemented after the vote at the AGM.

The first phase was to brief senior management and key communicators just ahead of the Stock Exchange announcement so that they could answer questions when the news broke. A helpline was set up at corporate head office to provide support for key communicators, as well as the early identification of any likely hurdles.

On the eve of the announcement, a special edition of *THF Times* was published and distributed during the night so that every member of staff would receive a copy the following morning. It was estimated that a success rate of 88.2 per cent was achieved among the 100,000 staff.

At the AGM, shareholders voted overwhelmingly to approve the changes. That afternoon, senior management met key communicators and all the special material was unveiled. The **Cascade Pack** was most comprehensive and 25,000 briefing packs were distributed. A video was produced in seven different languages for international employees. Presentations for overseas staff were held in Amsterdam, Paris and the USA.

Evaluation showed that the Cascade material reached over 75 per cent of employees. Staff groups were asked to score the relevance and enjoyment of the activity. The result was:

56% — very relevant
43% — fairly relevant
67% — quite enjoyable
32% — very enjoyable.

The total operating budget for the complete communications programme, including the launch conferences, research and design developments, was £220 000. Much of this was taken up with the production of all the material, which came to about £2.20 per member of staff. The low cost was due to the expertise and commitment in-house which helped to minimize the use of external agencies.

Comment

A good example of the meticulous planning essential to keep all the company's employees at home and overseas fully aware of the changes in the company structure and thus avoid unnecessary rumour and worry.

Case History 16
J H Dewhurst's staff relations programme

How a medium-sized company decided to use public relations policies to improve trust, confidence, self-esteem and job satisfaction among all its employees spread over 1000 butcher shops throughout the United Kingdom.

Research

Dewhurst, The Master Butchers, have over 1200 traditional butcher shops distributed throughout the UK, having acquired all its national and regional competitors. The shops vary in size and staffing and in some cases in trading style and name. The 4000 members of staff can be found in prestige shops with the Royal Warrant or in large market style units.

Dewhurst's staff are recruited mainly from school leavers, with few, if any, formal qualifications. As survival, not merely profitability, depends on a high level of craft skill, Dewhurst have developed a much respected training programme, recognized by the Institute of Meat and the National Council for Vocational Qualifications. All district and area managers have been promoted from the shop floor and most head office and board directors with operational responsibilities share that background and craft qualification. Dewhurst train over half of the qualified butchers in the UK but suffer severe losses as staff are attracted away by other retailers, packaging plants for supermarkets, or go into business for themselves.

Planning

In 1987, a public relations consultancy, Welbeck Golin/Harris was briefed to restructure the staff relations programme to meet the following objectives:

1. To develop trust and confidence in management.
2. To enhance the family business atmosphere of the company.
3. To develop self-esteem and job satisfaction in employees.

Welbeck approached the project with the aim of meeting the human needs of the individual members of staff as well as the trading imperatives of the company.

Execution

The agreed programme covered four main features:

1. **Staff magazine**

    The most direct means of communication to the staff was the quarterly *Dewhurst News*. Welbeck redesigned and enlivened the magazine which was renamed *Counterpoint*. Distribution was made to all serving and retired staff. This medium allowed management to explain current trading policies and to speak to staff in a more personal manner than via the standard management instruction memorandum. The remainder of the magazine could then be devoted to staff news and achievements as well as informative features on new legislation or industry developments.

2. **Developing trust and confidence in management**

   Positive statements on industry matters were issued regularly to the trade and national press, and spokesmen were offered to the media to ensure that Dewhurst were seen as industry leaders and that formal instructions issued by management were seen to have the approval of the industry as a whole. All qualified staff were provided with the leading trade paper *The Meat Trades Journal* free of charge.

   Particular efforts were made to foster the younger employees. Welbeck worked with the Marketing and Training departments to develop a training log book and to set up staff hostels as a 'home from home' for them whilst on training courses or on a tour of duty away from home.

3. **Enhancing the family business atmosphere**

   Steps were taken to ensure that long service or exemplary acts by staff were recognized by senior management, involving families where possible. For example, long service presentations were centred around a meal attended by the employee's family, close friends on the staff and hosted by a board director. News of these events and photographs were distributed as appropriate.

4. **Developing self-esteem and job satisfaction**

   The Young Butcher's Award Scheme was set up to provide recognition for young trainees. This resulted in substantial local and trade media coverage. When members of staff qualified as a Master Butcher, Dewhurst sponsored them for membership of the Institute of Meat and paid their subscription to *The Meat Trades Journal*. Staff were encouraged to serve on trade bodies such as the British Retail Association.

   All qualified butchers were entered for Dewhurst's Master Butcher of the Year Award which highlighted developments in refrigeration, labelling or ways of cutting and preparing meat. This scheme resulted in substantial local and trade media coverage. It has been restructured to make it more attractive and prestigious for competitors as well as to ensure that the tests and judging provided maximum media opportunities.

Evaluation

Staff levels have remained at agreed, adequate levels and recruiting new staff from school leavers has reached target levels.

A quality programme was prepared in late 1990 to survey the attitudes of all shop staff. The results were as follows:

Self-esteem and job satisfaction

97 per cent of staff agreed that they were satisfied with their job and promotion prospects.

88 per cent agreed that their contribution to Dewhurst was recognized adequately.

Trust/confidence objective

94 per cent agreed that they were definitely more inclined to have confidence in their management.

Enhancing the family atmosphere
97 per cent agreed that they would recommend a career with Dewhurst to a younger relative.

Summary
Dewhurst were very pleased with the success of the programme which will be continued.

Comment
This is a very different type of organization from Forte but the programme of good internal communication yielded equally satisfactory results. Morale and job satisfaction are essential ingredients of any profitable business.

Case history 17
Communications 2000 — two-way communication for the future

Rhône-Poulenc Ag Company (R-P Ag), a US operation of Rhône-Poulenc S.A., the largest French chemical company, recorded dynamic growth in the United States following a major acquisition in 1987. R-P Ag manufactures agricultural crop protection products and has 2600 employees at nine sites, plus field offices. Sites vary from seven to 1400 employees. Its headquarters is in Research Triangle Park, North Carolina.

The merging of corporate cultures and the parent company's French heritage left many employees with a need for a clearer understanding of the company's new culture and future. The situation was potentially unstable.

Overall objectives
The company had four clear objectives in planning a two-way communication programme which it called 'Communications 2000'. They were:

- to create an environment where employees could be more creative and productive;
- develop a strong corporate culture based on accepted values;
- to help management to be more responsive to employee needs;
- to be highly specific, budget conscious and to contribute in a tangible way to profitability.

Research
The purpose of the research was to establish benchmarks by combining a communication audit of the effectiveness of existing communication channels with a comprehensive look at employee opinions on job satisfaction issues such as the company's management style, culture and values and preparedness to meet any crisis.

Measurable research objectives
- Communication audit:
  to compare existing with desired sources of information;

to evaluate the credibility of sources;
to identify the information important to employees;
to measure the level of knowledge about company issues.
■ Employee–company issues:
to assess employee perceptions of community relations;
to evaluate R-P Ag culture and internal relationships;
to determine the awareness of company values.

Initial research

In January 1990, an in-depth communication survey was posted to all employees. The survey was designed to determine how employees perceive and relate to the company and to establish a benchmark for modifying existing communications or to develop new programmes to meet identified needs.

The employee response rate was 41 per cent, a very high return for such a complicated questionnaire. The results revealed serious problems with employee morale and internal communications. Employees felt they were not receiving the information they wanted about the company; they did not know company values; they felt managers were insensitive to their needs.

The research methodology used two innovative techniques: *semantic evaluation* to simplify the assimilation of qualitative data from many open-ended questions, and *force-field analysis* of the results to aid in strategic planning.

Programme planning and execution

Based on the research findings, the plans for Communications 2000 included:

1. Improving internal information systems to better meet employee needs by:

    — developing a new logo to give a dramatic and easily identifiable corporate message to all company publications;
    — revitalizing the company newsletter *AgCommunique* and making a distribution change by posting it to employee homes;
    — initiating *AgVisory* to help managers to be better conduits of information both from employees to senior management and vice versa;
    — designing a simple grid lay-out system for publications using desktop publishing equipment;
    — developing an editorial plan for all publications to ensure they respond to the priority information needs identified by the survey;
    — developing a protocol book to ensure consistency of publication.

2. Two new interactive programmes were introduced:
    — *'Lunch with . . .'* At headquarters, a senior executive has lunch once a month with a cross section of employees, followed by informal discussion.
    — *'La France et les Français'*. This is a French culture programme

held at headquarters to build bridges with their French parent company.

3. Values. The company focused on two activities to make company value better understood and applied by all employees:
   — using *AgCommunique* and *AgVisory* to discuss the values and present examples of employees 'living' the values in day-to-day operations;
   — training that links values with communication skills.

4. Addressing human relations issues. The Executive Management Committee has initiated an experimental work week schedule and a modification of summer working hours.

Evaluation of Communication 2000

- The company now has a detailed and reliable benchmark.
- Evaluation of employee communications. Readership studies measured the effectiveness of the revitalized *AgCommunique* and the newly established *AgVisory*. Follow-up research from a random sample of managers and employees indicated a more positive feeling about the publications. Both managers and employees said that *AgCommunique* now helped them to understand better the complex company history, its corporate values and its future direction and that their families read it.

  Managers said that *AgVisory* gave them a better idea of what was going on in other departments of R-P Ag and gave them information they could share with staff and helped them to answer questions.

- Interactive programmes.
  1. *La France et les Français* These events, presented by volunteers, draw 'standing room only' crowds and are eagerly attended by spouses and some members of the community.
  2. *'Lunch with . . .'* Initially designed for senior executives of R-P Ag based in the United States, this programme is now used to help bridge the cultural gulf between French executives and American employees. Attendee feedback forms are used to evaluate each session. On a scale of 0 to 5, meetings have averaged 4+.

  - Human relations issues. A survey on the modification of summer working hours gave 85 per cent approval. The compressed work week also received an 85 per cent satisfaction level.

Comment

The company was aware that the results of the arrival in the United States of the largest French chemical company presented a potentially unstable situation and this case history outlines the steps they took to avoid conflict.

Case history 18
Sending a daily newsletter to employees — AT & T

AT & T, the huge American communications giant, has employees in many different locations in many countries. Their ambition has been to devise a scheme whereby all really important company news could be given to employees internally at the same time as it is released to the external media. Employees would hear it first through internal sources — bulletins, publications, television or from a talk with the boss. An experiment started in January 1990 has proved very successful.

Taking advantage of the widespread availability and use of electronic mail throughout the company, they launched a daily electronic newsletter called *AT & T Today*. The objectives were threefold:

1. To provide timely information about the company and its competitors.
2. To deliver important news immediately and cost effectively.
3. To create credible, candid two-way communications through a letters section.

At the outset, they were not sure how many employees could be reached in this way. They wanted to reach not only those with access to the AT & T electronic service, but also to encourage pass-along readership through employees who would print out the daily newsletter and share it with others. Where employees could not be reached by electronic mail, the newsletter could be sent automatically to a fax machine.

The results surpassed expectations. The annual employee communication survey indicated that, after just two years, 130,000 AT & T employees read the newsletter three times a week or more. The regular users include more than half all management personnel. More than 80 per cent of employees say that *AT & T Today* provides timely, up-to-date information and useful company news.

The response to the 'letters to the editor' section has been especially interesting. Right from the beginning, it generated up to 40 letters a day. Employees want to be heard, and these letters have been remarkably straightforward and relevant to company issues. At the outset, senior officers of the company expressed concern — even dismay — at the items the public relations department published in the newsletter. However, they stuck to their principle of candour and an amazing thing happened. The *AT & T* senior management began to accept the letters section as a valid gauge — even an early warning system — of employee issues and concerns. They now regard it as a mini-survey that goes on continuously.

To support AT & T's growing international business, it was decided to begin developing regional editions of *AT & T Today* which will be followed by country specific editions. In each case, the local editor begins with the basic newsletter material from headquarters. He or she then adapts the basic material, translates it into the local language if necessary, and creates original material to reflect current news in that region or country. The local material is then sent to other editors around the world so that all versions of the newsletter can become increasingly global.

The public relations objective is a 24-hour window from the time news happens anywhere in the world to when it is received by employees everywhere in the world.

Comment

A telecommunications company has obvious advantages when it comes to communicating with employees but the principle is the same. Give as much information as possible, as quickly as can be managed and with clarity and lack of bias.

11
Crisis management

Disasters and crises are nothing new, but a number of particularly dramatic accidents during the last ten years have focused attention on this particular problem.

An accident or a disaster is primarily a management problem, but the event immediately becomes a media event, particularly if human death or injury is involved. The occurrence may have serious repercussions for the company concerned: it may even threaten the future existence of the company. Thus crisis management immediately involves crisis public relations.

Crises usually blow up suddenly and spread with amazing rapidity. Often they occur at night or at weekends or holidays. Thus there is an obvious need for appropriate planning so that immediate action can be implemented. Every crisis is different, however, and even carefully laid plans require constant re-evaluation and updating.

'Known unknowns' and 'unknown unknowns'

Potential crises can be classified as *known unknowns* and *unknown unknowns*. In industries such as the railways, airlines, shipping, chemicals, nuclear power, oil refining, electricity generation, pipelines, coal mining, construction and tunnelling it is quite possible that disaster will strike at some time. The danger is 'known' but if or when it may happen is 'unknown'. Apart from accidents likely to involve loss of life, there are other possible crises of a financial nature, such as hostile take-over bids, computer fraud, death of the chairman, or liquidation of suppliers or debtors.

If an organization is potentially vulnerable to such known unknowns it is imperative that careful planning be undertaken before it becomes necessary. 'Be prepared' must be the official policy.

Unknown unknowns present a different scenario. This group of crises cannot reasonably be foreseen. It includes so-called acts of God such as earthquakes, volcanic eruptions or floods but increasingly it includes criminal acts such as the poisoning of drugs or food in a supermarket. A number of cases of contamination of food have been reported and the perpetrators sent to prison but it is likely that many cases go unreported as manufacturers are afraid of copycat crimes. It is difficult to see how plans can be formulated in advance to meet such emergencies, but immediate reaction is essential if such a crisis erupts.

Computer fraud is another increasing threat to business and strenuous efforts are being made to contain its effect.

Preparing a crisis plan

Planning to react to a possible emergency is fairly straightforward once the decision to prepare has been taken and has received management approval.

There are six stages that require attention.

1. **Analyzing possibilities of trouble**
    In considering proposals for drawing up a crisis plan and preparing to train staff, it is obviously wise to carry out a careful assessment of likely problems. This is necessary in order to convince management that the proposals are reasonable and necessary. After this analysis, a written assessment can be produced which must be approved formally by management.
2. **Preparing a plan**
    Once the initial analysis and proposals have been approved by management, the next stage is to prepare a detailed plan to meet all potential threats.
3. **Staff selection**
    Many individual members of staff are required to form a rota of men and women who will be available should disaster strike. The main need would be for people to man the telephones and to deal with the calls from the media which can run into thousands if the crisis is serious and involving loss of life. Experience has shown that secretaries are usually best suited to cope with this exacting work. In drawing up a rota, it is necessary to bear in mind the need for 24-hour coverage. Crises have a perverse habit of occurring at night or during holidays or weekends.
4. **Communication facilities**
    Careful consideration must be given to means of coping with the heavy demands on communication links under actual crisis conditions. It may be possible to arrange to share telephones and fax facilities with other nearby companies. If the company has consultants they may be called upon to deal with media.
5. **Training**
    The designated staff will need training to ensure that they are fully equipped to meet requirements should an accident occur.

6. **Practice simulation exercises**

Unannounced practice exercises should be held at irregular intervals with cooperation from the police and other local authorities. If these exercises are to be valuable and to yield useful information, it is essential that they should be as realistic as possible. If a video is made of the whole exercise, it can be replayed later and discussed by those who took part. This can be a valuable training resource. Figure 11.1 illustrates the different groups involved in a crisis.

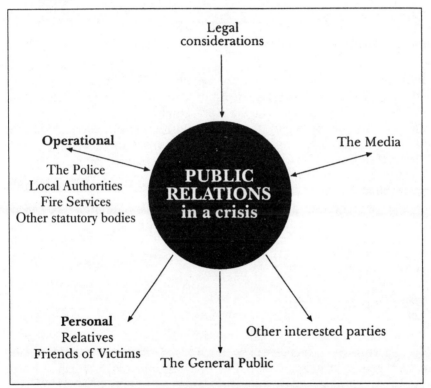

Figure 11.1 *Illustrating the different groups involved in a crisis*

All these preparations may appear to be overkill, but if an organization is in a vulnerable field, the results of lack of preparation can be catastrophic. There are a number of very large companies in the UK and overseas who have disappeared completely through very bad handling of crises which hit them.

To sum up, there are four ways to turn a crisis into an opportunity:

1. Adequate preparation. Drawing up a plan. Training staff. Providing ample communication links.

2. Implementing plans which have been well designed and regularly tested.
3. Dealing with the media who will seek instant news and explanations.
4. Paying attention to the anxieties of relatives and friends by providing dedicated telephone lines for enquiries.

It is comforting to believe that a crisis plan, constantly re-evaluated and refined, will enable an organization to deal with any sudden emergency. It is certain that a plan will provide a better chance of avoiding difficulties with the media but experience has shown that every crisis tends to raise different problems.

Preparations

In drawing up a crisis plan, logistics and physical requirements will need attention. On the media side, it is useful to prepare technical data sheets which can be handed out to media representatives to provide background information and to satisfy them until positive information about the incident is available. If all this background data can be filed in a ring binder (fast fact book), with a good index, and kept up to date, it will prove invaluable in answering media enquiries in the early days (or minutes) when there is little hard news to give out.

The preparations and detailed advance planning must be taken seriously if it is to be really useful should an incident occur. The initiative for the crisis management preparations is likely to come from the public relations department but the planning will require the active participation of many departments.

Reacting to disaster

If preparations have been made satisfactorily, the immediate problem of dealing with an emergency will be much easier and less frantic. However, certain general principles should be followed in every instance:

1. Immediate reaction to media enquiries is essential.
2. Only known facts should be given out. Guesses about likely causes or casualties must be avoided at all costs.
3. It is desirable to call a general news conference as soon as sufficient hard news is available for dissemination. As full information as possible should be given out at the conference and all relevant questions answered.
4. If at all possible, the chairman or chief executive officer should preside at the news conference. It creates a very bad impression if a senior member of management does not come to the scene of an accident to meet the media and to answer questions. The choice of

the main spokesperson at the press conference, however, deserves some thought as his or her speech and general demeanour will have a strong effect on the television viewing audience.

5. An opportunity to gain some advantage from an unfortunate accident arises from the way in which relatives of the dead or injured are treated. This is an occasion for hospitality to be extended without stint and for maximum sensitivity to be exercised. If a lawyer is present, there may be pressure on the company to avoid any expression of sympathy lest this be taken to imply liability. Any suggestion of this kind must be resisted and in some circumstances the offer of *ex gratia* payments may be part of the way in which sympathy can be expressed in practical terms. Lawyers must be told that the consequences to the company of *not* communicating and showing sympathy in practical terms are sure to be much worse than if an open policy of full information and generosity is adopted.

The Chernobyl incident

Even among many very serious accidents in recent years, the nuclear disaster at Chernobyl in 1986 stands out. The effect on public opinion world-wide was heightened by the initial secrecy which engendered exaggerated rumours about the effects of the nuclear discharges. At the Public Relations World Congress at Melbourne in April 1988 a professor from Moscow University spoke about the disaster at Chernobyl and admitted their errors in handling the emergency. He said that in future there would be a public relations expert attached to every major utility.

Dow Canada's crisis policy

Dow Canada are continually sending chemicals across Canada by train and when occasionally there is a railway accident Dow Canada have a crisis on their hands. The company maintains a crisis team ready to fly anywhere in Canada at a minute's notice. Dow's policy can be summarized under five headings:

1. Honesty first, foremost and always.
2. Empathy and compassion.
3. Openness, accessibility and candour.
4. Timeliness.
5. Proactive, not simply reactive.

The record of Dow Canada in responding positively and rapidly to cases of potential contamination following rail accidents is an excellent one. A recent case, however, has shown that it is not enough to deal correctly with the media but it is also important to monitor carefully how the media reports the occurrence. It is the local community which is at risk, so direct contact with local residents is advisable to forestall possible protests and demonstrations.

The Exxon Valdez disaster

After Chernobyl, the running aground of the *Exxon Valdez* in King William Sound off the Alaskan coast was the biggest environmental disaster in recent years. This typical example of a known unknown — a disaster waiting to happen — occurred in the middle of the night on Good Friday, 24 March 1989. It is remarkable how often accidents happen during the night or at holiday time.

The initial fine weather did not last and the problem was aggravated by the onset of high winds. By 15 April, nine million gallons of oil had been spilt into the sea covering an area of over 500 square miles, and causing the death of an estimated 500,000 birds and countless seals and whales.

Permission to build the pipeline and to ship oil through King William Sound, one of the purest nature habitats in North America, had been granted to Alyeska, a consortium of oil companies, on condition that they would be able to cope quickly and adequately with any possible disaster. A film, 'Disaster at Valdez', has recently had a wide screening. It shows how the consequences of the accident were aggravated and compounded by lack of resources and arguments between the oil company, the US Coastguard and the Alaskan Department of Environment about the correct way to deal with the emergency.

A crisis management plan might not have had much effect on such a major accident but its preparation and rehearsals would have uncovered and drawn attention to the need for adequate resources to be readily available with agreed contingency action plans.

Tailpiece: There is now a new battle over how the compensation money of over $1000 billion is to be allocated among the interests involved and spent to best advanatage.

Disaster in the air

British Airways and British Midland are two of the British companies which have taken crisis management very seriously.

The accident in which a British Midland plane crashed on the M1 Motorway in 1989 occurred only a little while after the company had staged a disaster rehearsal. This may have helped the company deal with the crisis in a manner which inspired public confidence. Michael Bishop, the British Midland chairman, was quickly on the scene and showed appropriate concern and sympathy with the relatives of the dead and all others affected by the accident.

British Airways also make extensive preparations to cope with any sudden crisis and have an emergency procedures information centre (EPIC) at Heathrow. EPIC is operated by British Airways and is available to about 40 subscribing airlines operating in the UK. It is located in the basement of the Queen's Building at Heathrow and forms part of the British Airways Crisis Management Centre.

The level of safety in aviation is very high in relation to the millions of passenger miles flown. However, when an accident involving an aircraft does occur the results can be sensational. The human complexity of a modern air disaster and the world-wide interest it usually attracts demands a high level of preparedness. EPIC was designed to meet this need and has been steadily refined in the light of experience. Training is provided for subscribing airlines and should an accident occur the Centre can provide all the facilities required, manned by trained British Airways staff working in conjunction with the police and other authorities involved.

British Airways has not had to use the resources of EPIC itself recently but the Centre has played a key role in a number of accidents. The Lockerbie disaster was the largest incident it has been called upon to deal with. EPIC was operational within 25 minutes of the Pan Am flight disappearing off the radar screen and remained actively involved for ten days. Less than a month later, the Centre was again alerted to cope with the British Midland crash. Four thousand calls were received and dealt with during the first 24 hours.

EPIC thus performs a very valuable dual function: helping airlines to prepare for any emergency and active involvement should the worst occur.

Man-made contamination

As if there were not enough natural and unavoidable disasters in the world, in November 1982 the United States suffered the first example of deliberate tampering with food and drugs on the shelves of shops in the high street.

It happened in Chicago. The target was *Tylenol* headache capsules made by Johnson & Johnson which had 35 per cent of the market in the US. The scare started with three deaths attributed to cyanide poisoning. Johnson & Johnson reacted immediately by recalling millions of bottles of its extra strength headache capsules. The company also spent about

$500,000 on informing doctors, hospitals and distributors of the possible dangers. After testing seven million tablets, the company found that only 75 capsules had been poisoned, all from the same batch.

After a suitable interval, Johnson & Johnson reissued *Tylenol* in tamper resistant packaging and their bold action in recalling all supplies of the drug has proved profitable in the long run as the drug soon regained its position as market leader. The perpetrator of the poisoning was never found.

Unfortunately, this well publicized crime led to a rash of copycat cases of contamination or threatened contamination in many countries including Britain. In September 1989, a Dundee man was jailed for five years for trying to extort £600,000 from supermarkets and consumer goods manufacturers. Another man was sent to prison for five years for attempting to extort £140,000 from Marks and Spencer. Similar attempts at blackmail occurred in other parts of the UK.

This was followed by even more serious incidents. One case was Heinz baby foods which were contaminated with different items including caustic soda and razor blades. Another serious case was the contamination of HP baked beans. It is not known how many cases of this kind have occurred but all manufacturers have increased their vigilance.

The example of Johnson & Johnson faced with the *Tylenol* problem has shown that prompt action is the best way to deal with emergencies of this kind.

Summary

There are many different kinds of possible crises which may hit a company or organization but the fundamental rules for dealing with emergencies apply equally to all: the details naturally will depend on circumstances and the nature of the crisis.

The following nine rules are based on the experience of companies facing emergencies of many different kinds:

1. React immediately and activate the organization's crisis management plan.
2. Try to get your chairman or chief executive officer to come to the scene of the incident as quickly as possible.
3. Tell the media as much as possible, but stick strictly to *known* facts, do not make guesses about the cause of the crisis or about casualties.
4. Have background information readily available to feed to the media until the facts of the incident can be stated with confidence.
5. Treat sympathetically relatives and friends of victims. Publicize special dedicated telephone numbers which can be telephoned by those seeking information about possible casualties.

6. Call a news conference as soon as there is positive news to impart. Make sure that the room used is suitable. It needs to be large enough to accommodate all the local and national media represenatives and it is helpful if there is more than one exit so that the speakers can leave at the end of the conference without the possibility of being mobbed by the journalists.
7. Endeavour to have your chairman or chief executive officer at the press conference.
8. Try to avoid too many technicalities and above all, do not give any indication that you are trying to blind the media with science. Make it absolutely clear that you are very sorry about what has happened and are taking every possible step to set matters right.
9. Remember that the interest of the media may persist for a long time. Critical press comment may erupt long after the event and may have to be answered.

Case history 19
The purity of water — Perrier

The growing sales world-wide of Perrier and other bottled waters was due to the public belief that, whereas tap water might or might not be safe to drink, bottled water could be relied upon for purity and absence of contaminants. It came as a shock, therefore, when it was announced that traces of benzene had been found in bottles of Perrier.

Weak concentrations of metals and other chemicals are found naturally in many foods and, indeed, some of these trace elements are needed for good health. The main basis of the remarkable increase in the consumption of bottled water, about 35 per cent per year world-wide, however, was the consumers' belief in its absolute purity. As market leader, this was particularly true of Perrier in the United States, one of its main markets where the company's advertising slogan was: '*It's perfect, It's Perrier*'.

The start of the problem came about because some American scientists in Charlotte, North Carolina were in the habit of using bottles of Perrier water when they needed purified water for their experiments. It was easier than making their own. On 19 January, 1991 they discovered that the 'pure water' they had purchased in a green Perrier bottle contained minute quantities of benzene, an industrial solvent and a carcinogen. The laboratory findings were confirmed by the US Food and Drug Administration (FDA) and while the concentration of benzene in the bottled water was well below a level that might endanger health it was well above the limit permitted by the FDA.

When the Perrier Group of America heard about the problem in early February they acted very quickly by recalling over 70,000 bottles from shops and restaurants in North America. In France, Source Perrier acted decisively by halting all bottling of the mineral water.

The initial reaction was fine but then all the mistakes started. On February 11, a Source Perrier spokesman stated that the source of the benzene in the bottled water had come from a cleaning fluid used on the bottling line which served the North American market. The statement went on to say that the machine in question had been removed from the bottling line and the source of Perrier at Vergeze, in the South of France, was unaffected by any pollutants. This was mistake number one: never guess at the cause of a crisis or invent an explanation. At this date, Perrier had no idea of the cause of the contamination.

Several days later, the real cause of the trouble was discovered. Company employees had failed to replace charcoal filters used to screen out impurities in the natural gas present in the source. This simple carelessness resulted in the loss of the whole production for six months. On 14 February, only four days after the discovery, the Perrier chairman announced the total recall of Perrier water world-wide but joked about the problem to the assembled journalists who were crammed into a small room — and served with Perrier water.

Unlike its French head office, the Perrier British subsidiary acted much more responsibly. The chairman, Wenche Marshall-Foster, had realized years earlier that any suggestion of contamination could ruin Perrier's sales in the United Kingdom and had set up a four-member crisis management team. The result was that the crisis management team was able to go into action immediately and the crisis was dealt with effectively in the United Kingdom. The team was to be found in Perrier's London offices for days talking to anyone affected by the problem. They told the media that they did not know the cause of the trouble until the facts had been established. The media responded to this candour. To reassure Perrier drinkers, the company took full page advertisements in the newspapers stating that there was 'no hazard' to health.

Deprived of supplies for six weeks, many customers found that other brands of mineral water were good alternatives. Both in the US and the United Kingdom, Perrier's market share has dropped and only in France has it held its own. Professor Stephen A Greyser, of the Harvard University Graduate School of Business Administration, commented that the public could forgive Johnson & Johnson for the poison in *Tylenol* as it was not their fault. Perrier, however, had caused the contamination and had appeared to try to cover it up. Perrier's relaunch in the United States also ran into difficulties, with the FDA objecting to some of the statements on the bottle labels. The wording had to be changed before selling Perrier in the US could be resumed.

Comparison between the recommendations in this chapter and the way in which Perrier acted when disaster struck are ample confirmation of the importance of planning ahead and making plans to meet any sudden emergency.

Writing in *Prism*, a journal published by Arthur D Little, the management consultants, Ashok Kalelkar and John Magee commented: 'Managers tend to be wrong-footed in corporate crises because they are used to shaping events, not to having events grasp control and shape them. The *Economist* wrote on August 3 1991: 'Once it had regained control of the affair — a week long struggle — Perrier did most things right. But it would all have been a lot easier had each part of the company been pouring from the same bottle at the outset'.

Comment

This case history emphasizes the importance of liaison between national subsidiaries of a multinational company. Had the French head office been aware of the British concern with crisis management, and had followed their example, the benzene incident could have been coped with in an orderly manner and without the difficulties that actually arose.

Case history 20
Rebuilding public trust — BF Goodrich

Concern about potential health and safety risks of chemical products has grown significantly in recent years, particularly in the communities where they are manufactured. This problem has been compounded in the United States by new regulations that require chemical companies to report publicly on any accidental releases or spills.

The BFGoodrich Company at its Avon Lake facility in Ohio, USA was preparing a plan that would help the local community to understand better the company's performance under these new laws when a series of incidents thrust it into the media spotlight and created a public outcry.

Background

Located just beyond Greater Cleveland, the BFGoodrich Avon Lake complex has served as one of the company's most strategically important manufacturing and research sites since 1946. For the most part, the facility's relationship with Avon Lake has been harmonious, except for a period in the 70s when a link was discovered between prolonged high exposure to one of the materials used on site and a certain type of cancer. This issue was resolved, but new regulations created by the US Government in 1986 threatened to raise unfounded concerns about the plant.

By 1988, these new regulations required increased reporting which made it look as if BFG's environmental performance was declining. The potential for negative backlash was obvious and in 1988 the site formed a steering committee to help communicate BFG's performance under the new law in correct perspective. Before this effort could take effect however, a series of incidents at the site generated extensive negative media coverage, increased public scrutiny and compelled the steering committee to formulate a broader programme targeted to key audiences. In early 1989, the committee's efforts began to reap some initial results. However, that progress halted abruptly in June when an out of date report on national cancer risks gained local media coverage and an additional incident at the facility further exacerbated public concern.

The company retained local public relations counsel, Edward Howard & Company, and the site's community relations committee began to develop a fully fledged community relations programme to rebuild the public's trust in BFG.

Research

Although recent events had clearly had a negative impact on public opinion towards BFG, a full assessment of the situation had not taken place. A comprehensive enquiry established the facts and provided the background needed to build a full communication programme.

On the company's side, there was great frustration that the true story was not being told or accepted, although BFG's claim of environmental commitment could be substantiated. It seemed that their publicity and publications were a good foundation for increased communication efforts but that new material should be simplified and expressed in layman's terms.

Planning

In August 1989, the Steering Committee's plans were incorporated into a larger programme that included overall objectives and strategies. The objectives were identified as:

- enhancing the facility's image by building understanding about its safe operating procedures and its firm commitment to being a good corporate citizen;
- defusing concerns about perceived hazards by building understanding of what is done on site, and how materials are handled and disposed of;
- building a solid base of community support to help facilitate future expansion, to undermine 'fringe element' crusades against the facility and to guard against unfair criticism in the future.

Six groups were identified as target audiences: local media, local government officials, Avon Lake schools, local service and industrial groups, the company's employees and the general population of Avon Lake.

Programme strategy

There were four main strands to the strategy:

1. Be open, honest and straightforward.
2. Get key audiences personally familiar with the works and its operation.
3. Put the site's operations in friendly terms by emphasizing end products made from the plant's materials.
4. Use non-technical language to describe the activities.

The new plan included 11 major areas of activity designed to build relationships with the key audiences. A budget was approved for this extra public relations activity and a special budget for the 1990 Community Open House event.

Implementation

Throughout 1990 and 1991, the committee pursued all the different strands of the programme and a number of new special initiatives were undertaken.

Attendance at the Community Open House exceeded 5500 and follow-up research found very positive results on community opinion.

The Schools Partnership Programme included 200 student tours, 25 'shadowing' experiences and 50 classroom presentations in the first year.

The Speakers Bureau received increased requests and steps were taken to improve this service.

Earth Day 1990 was supported by community and employee projects and good media coverage resulted.

Evaluation

BFGoodrich established this public relations programme at Avon Lake to address the natural concern of the community about having a chemical manufacturing complex in its midst. The overall objective was to improve public attitudes towards the plant and in less than two years the company was satisfied that it had achieved substantial improvements. By using honest, straightforward communication, BFG Avon Lake had been able to reduce substantially local community's fears and to rebuild the public's trust in its operations.

Comment

This open communication approach, which worked successfully at Avon Lake, is a model that applies not only to the world-wide chemical industry, but to any company or industry seeking to strengthen its community relations.

12

The management and organization of public relations

The management of public relations does not have any unique features. To be successful, whether practised in-house or in a consultancy, public relations must follow effective business methods applicable to similar occupations which combine counselling with the provision of services.

Effective time management is very important as many activities are time sensitive. This applies particularly to media relations and the production of annual reports and other publications such as house journals.

The introduction of information technology into the work place has brought with it new opportunities for automation which can speed up and expand many aspects of information gathering and communication transmission. There are now available a bewildering variety of computer based information services which can be used for research and other purposes. Many different databases can be accessed and this aids the preparation of programmes. For example, it is possible to research from your office desk, back issues of the *Economist* or foreign newspapers like *Handelsblatt*. The same computer equipment can also be used for electronic mail and routine office procedures such as time sheets and general accounting. One hesitates to make prophecies but it is fairly safe to predict that information technology will have increasing effect on public relations procedures in a number of different areas such as research, monitoring, national and international communication, delivery of news, and evaluation.

It is not likely, however, that the introduction of electronic aids will diminish the use of conventional methods and media. Experience has shown that as new media such as radio and television have become established they supplement but do not oust earlier media such as print.

Models of public relations practice

Professor James Grunig, of the University of Maryland, has tried to describe all the different methods of public relations practice under four models. In *Managing Public Relations* which Grunig wrote with T. Hunt (published by Holt Rhinehart Winston, 1984) it is suggested that by considering these four models it is possible to understand better the history of public relations, how it has developed and how it can be practised to best advantage.

The four models are: press agentry/publicity, public information, two-way asymmetric, and two-way symmetric. It is suggested that 15 per cent of organizations use press agentry/publicity; 50 per cent use public information; 20 per cent use two-way asymmetric; and only 15 per cent use two-way symmetric methodology. These estimated percentages relate to the US but they would probably be rather similar for the UK and other developed countries.

Grunig explains that in the first two models, communication is always one-way, from the organization to publics. Practitioners of these two models generally view their function as talking, not listening. These first two models differ, however, in that the press agentry/publicists do not always feel obligated to present a complete picture of the organization or product they represent, whereas public information specialists do.

For the two-way asymmetric and two-way symmetric practitioners, communication flows both to and from publics but there is a big difference in the nature of this two-way communication. The two-way asymmetric model is 'asymmetric' because the effects of the public relations are imbalanced in favour of the organization. The organization does not change as a result of public opinion; it attempts to change public attitudes and behaviour. Two-way symmetric practitioners carefully plan what they communicate to publics to achieve maximum change in attitude and behaviour. This model consists more of a dialogue than a monologue.

Grunig argues very strongly that only under the fourth model can excellence in public relations practice be achieved.

The four model theory is useful in describing the various aspects of public relations practice, but why must these four models be mutually exclusive? Most comprehensive public relations programmes are likely to include elements of all four models. A comparison with the medical profession illustrates this point. A doctor may choose general practice or become a physician or a surgeon. One specialist may choose dermatology or paediatrics while another may concentrate on delicate brain surgery. Nobody would suggest that these are different models of practice. Surely they are all equally part of medical practice.

A medical student passes examinations and after a period of professional experience qualifies as a doctor. Similarly, a student can take a BA Honours degree in public relations and after a period of experience qualify for full membership of the Institute of Public Relations. Neither a medical student nor a public relations student comes out of education as a fully qualified practitioner. A considerable amount of professional practice is necessary to produce a rounded and experienced practitioner.

While accepting that Grunig's fourth model of public relations is the ideal, it is more reasonable to argue that all four models can be practised within the same programme, not necessarily at the same time but using the appropriate method to meet different requirements.

Grunig has quoted from a research project which he has been undertaking with some colleagues for the International Association of Business Communicators. He categorizes excellence of public relations programmes under the following headings.

1. **Micro level**
   1.1 Managed strategically.
   1.2 Separate function from marketing.
   1.3 Direct reporting relationship to senior management.

2. **Managerial level**
   2.1 A single or integrated public relations department.
   2.2 Two-way symmetrical model.
   2.3 Senior public relations person in the managerial role.
   2.4 Potential for excellent public relations, as indicated by:
       a) knowledge of symmetrical model;
       b) knowledge of managerial role;
       c) academic training in public relations;
       d) professionalism.

3. **Macro level**
   3.1 Public relations director has power in or with the dominant coalition.
   3.2 Participative rather than authoritarian organizational culture.
   3.3 Systematic system of internal communication.
   3.4 Organic rather than mechanical organizational structure.
   3.5 Turbulent, complex environment with pressure from activist groups.

4. **Effects of excellent public relations**
   4.1 Micro-level origrammes meet communication objectives.
   4.2 At the macro level, reduces costs of regulation, pressure and litigation.
   4.3 Job satisfaction is high among employees.

Grunig contends that excellence can only exist in a two-way symmetrical programme. Another way of assessing excellence, however, is to suggest that a measure of excellence is when evaluation and perception exceed expectation consistently. In practice, it is equally possible to achieve high quality and excellence in any of the four different Grunig models which may be operating concurrently in a public relations programme.

Some aspects of excellence and quality

When Professor Tim Traverse-Healy addressed the First European Conference on Quality and Management in Business Services in December 1990, he outlined these concepts as they relate particularly to public relations practice.

Practitioners in any professional discipline, understand and subscribe to agreed ethical standards and act with integrity towards their clients, past and present, and towards their colleagues and their competitors. For public relations, this has additional dimensions. It is also necessary to protect the integrity of the media of communication, the elected and appointed representatives of the community, and with the public at large. Ethics and integrity in this connection encompass such issues as truth, the encouragement of true dialogue and concern for the public interest. Furthermore, the rights of freedom of expression cover such topics as accountability, disclosure, social responsibility and corporate governance, and focus on the duty to protect from corruption the avenues of communication and the processes of democracy.

These aspects of professional conduct are enshrined in the codes adopted by the Institute of Public Relations and similar national bodies, and which are mandatory on all members.

Traverse-Healy summarized the requirements of excellence in consultancy practice as follows:

1. Excellence in consultancy

- The extent of in-house experience and the track record of individual directors and senior executives.
- The quality and experience of the second tier of management and the essential support staff.
- Present clients and the strength of past and present relationships.
- The commercial stability and viability of the agency.
- Its record of staff turnover.
- Its investment in careful recruitment, staff training and executive education.
- The contribution of the executives to professional affairs and to fresh thinking.
- Commitment to fundamental research and investment in new technology.
- Commitment to and involvement with the professional associations and strict adherence to their codes of professional conduct.

2. Excellence in professional service quality

- The existence of an in-house published statement of corporate mission and operating principles

- Established procedures for the regular review of the consultancy's advice, plans and work on behalf of individual clients.
- The in-house process whereby opinions or matters of client concern are debated, articulated and promulgated.
- The extent to which subjects are researched prior to recommendations being made.
- The methodology under which critical corporate self-analysis is carried out and progress and performance checked.
- The degree to which clear objectives and specific targets and performance benchmarks are agreed and progress monitored.
- The knowledge and use of evaluation and measurement techniques including opinion and attitudinal research.

To achieve excellence is very difficult, but Traverse-Healy's lists can be a target at which to aim. He has obviously focused his review on consultancy public relations as he would like to see it practised in Britain, but most of the items relate equally to in-house practice.

The following section of this chapter discusses the relative advantages and disadvantages of in-house and consultancy methods of providing public relations services, but these considerations are mainly of an organizational nature. The quality of the service provided by both methods should reach as near excellence as possible. Before completing this section, it may be informative to quote some historic relevant statements.

The late Sir Stephen Tallents, KCMG, founder president of the Institute of Public Relations stated:

I regard public relations work in its widest sense as one of the most far-reaching and important tasks of our time. I know it also, properly conducted, for a task requiring not only as much organizing ability as any straightforward administration or business, but demanding also an element of flair and a capacity to understand and work with artists.

Harold Burson, chairman of Burson-Marsteller, has supported the two-way symmetrical model in the following terms:

The public relations executive provides a qualitative evaluation of social trends. He helps formulate policies that will enable a corporation to adapt to these trends. And he communicates — both internally and externally — the reasons for these policies. One obvious objective for the public relations practitioner in the corporate environment is to make sure that business institutions perform as servants of the people.

James Grunig and other researchers in the United States will continue to pursue their studies of the various models which they believe will help us to understand the parameters of public relations practice, but in the meantime it is hoped that all aspects of public relations practice will be practised in a manner which aspires to excellence, conforms to accepted codes of professional conduct and encourages a high level of business and personal ethics.

Practice in-house or by consultancies

Previous chapters have discussed the different ways in which public relations practice makes an effective contribution to the success of organizations in both the proactive and reactive modes. It has been emphasized that public relations should always be an integral part of management and not regarded as a luxury. In a small organization, the chief executive or proprietor should regard public relations as part of the requirement of running the company. Even if there is a natural aptitude, however, it is likely that professional guidance will be required. In a larger organization, it is desirable for the chief executive officer or chairman to regard public relations as a vital part of managerial responsibilities and opportunities, and to see that its potential is exploited to the full.

However keen or qualified the chief executive is personally in the field of public relations, it will be necessary to have an in-house public relations department or to engage the services of a public relations consultancy to ensure that a planned and consistent public relations policy is initiated and maintained. The difference is self-evident. An in-house public relations department is similar to other departments of the company, but like other departments has certain special features and requirements. An outside consultancy works like any other kind of consultant, advising and carrying out agreed public relations activities for fees which may be based on a retainer or a time basis, or a combination of these two methods.

Public relations carried out in-house or through a consultancy are not mutually exclusive. Many companies employ a combination of the two methods, for a number of reasons. An in-house department may be large enough to meet average demands but not equipped to deal with special events or crises. A consultancy can be brought in to meet these overloads. Alternatively top management may consider that there are possible advantages in bringing in an outside point of view from time to time.

The quality of public relations service depends on the experience and ability of those carrying out the work; not on whether it is planned and executed inside or outside a company. When a consultancy is employed, it is necessary to judge the experience of those executives who will actually be working for the client. There are inherent advantages and disadvantages between the two methods of organizing public relations and it is worth considering these in some detail.

Advantages and disadvantages of in-house practice

There are five major advantages of an in-house department:

1. The head of public relations must have regular and direct access to top management and this is obviously easier when they are all in the same headquaters.
2. The staff are better equipped to answer media enquiries quickly and to seek additional information from other departments if necessary.
3. Being members of the staff, they are able to circulate freely within the opportunity to sense morale and to anticipate problems. These contacts are particularly helpful in planning and implementing internal relations programmes.
4. The staff become identified with the aims and objects of the organization and have a personal stake in its success.
5. If the size of the company warrants it, economy and efficiency can be increased by having separate subsections to deal with media relations, public affairs, exhibitions, publications etc.

These advantages are moderated to a certain extent by some intrinsic real disadvantages:

1. There is a tendency to underestimate the expertise of those with whom one is familiar.
2. The members of staff may become somewhat set in their thinking and ideas.
3. Opportunity to secure promotion and better remuneration may be hindered by management's desire to maintain parity with other senior employees.
4. There is a tendency to unload 'odd jobs' on the public relations department.

Advantages of employing consultants

There are four major advantages of consultants compared with in-house:

1. The principals of the consultancy are independent and can thus give unbiased counsel. There is also a strong, but often misguided tendency to respect advice from outsiders in preference to equally good, or better advice from within.
2. The executives engaged on the account are also working on other types of public relations for other clients and this broadens their experience.
3. The cost of the service is known accurately in advance and bears a direct relationship to the agreed programme and work commissioned. The budget can be varied easily from time to time and there are no social welfare or fringe benefit commitments.

4. If the results do not appear to reach the desired levels, it is easy to give notice to terminate or amend the existing contract by giving the appropriate notice.

On the downside, there can be disadvantages:

1. An outside firm is unlikely to have a detailed knowledge of the operations of the company and its day-to-day activities and thus needs careful briefing on appointment and at every new development. Regular consultation is essential and failure in this respect is the most common cause of dissatisfaction leading to termination of contract.
2. Media enquiries which are not factual or simple to answer, have to be referred for guidance and this precludes the speedy response which is so important in media relations.
3. There may be a lack of continuity, as staff in a consultancy are liable to leave or to be assigned to other accounts.

Selecting the ideal arrangement

Enough has been said to emphasize that there can be no simple choice between organizing public relations activities in-house or through the use of an outside consultancy. The decision will depend on the administrative planning of the company but also very much on experience and personal preference.

The ideal relationship is more difficult to decide when a large organisation has a central headquarters and a number of factories or subsidiary companies. While it is obviously important that public relations advice should be readily available to top management at the headquarters, it is also clear that many public relations proactive opportunities will be lost if there are not staff present at each centre to deal with requirements.

The personal preference of the chairman or the CEO can lead to changes in the planning. One recalls a large British company which had a comprehensive publicity and public relations office in central London in the headquarters building. A new chairman changed this arrangement. The central public relations facility was reduced to a very small level and asked to provide counselling, while public relations consultants were engaged to deal with the day-to-day practical requirements. The next chairman of the company reversed the process. A few years later, yet another new chairman changed the arrangements back again and this change has persisted.

The method of organizing the public relations function in an organization should not affect the efficiency of the service provided. This will depend on the ability and experience of the men and women carrying out the various aspects of public relations and the extent to which they are permitted to make their maximum contribution. This is equally true of practitioners working in-house or through a consultancy.

The organization of the public relations function is more complex for companies with overseas subsidiaries or foreign interests. The usual solution is to control public relations policy from headquarters but to operate it locally. The ideal should be: 'plan globally but act locally'. This subject is discussed in more detail in Chapter 13 which discusses international public relations and networking. Should an organization need advice on setting up a public relations department or engaging the services of public relations consultants, there are two reliable sources of information:

> The Institute of Public Relations. The Old Trading House, 15 Northburgh Street, London, EC1V 0PR. Telephone: 071–253 5151.

> The Public Relations Consultants Association, Willow House, Willow Place London SWIP 1JH. Telephone: 071–233 6026.

For information about public relations practice internationally, the best source is The International Public Relations Association, Case postale 2100, Ch- 1211, Geneva 2, Switzerland. Telephone: 22 791 0550.

13
Business ethics

The question of ethics in public relations is only a small part of the wider question of business ethics and ethical behaviour in the modern world. General moral principles may seem rather far removed from the day-to-day workings of business or public relations, nevertheless there is growing evidence of their relevance.

A company's mission statement should give guidance on ethical behaviour as it is mandatory within the organization. The concept of ethical and moral values within a company must be reflected down from the top. A report of the Institute of Personnel Management in 1992 revealed that mission statements have been published by three out of four of the largest British companies, and by 70 per cent of those in the public sector, yet only one in three of the organizations with mission statements had communicated them to all their employees.

When public relations practitioners discuss ethics, there is usually agreement that business can only operate successfully in a free society. The consensus is that full notice must always be taken of the 'public interest'. So what *is* the public interest? Walter Lippman described it thus: 'The public interest may be presumed to be what men would choose if they saw clearly, thought rationally, acted disinterestedly and benevolently'. He wrote this in 1955 but it is difficult to think of a better definition. Many situations are covered of course, by law and others by various types of regulatory bodies. This still leaves a very wide spectrum of situations and modes of behaviour which are not covered by any of these formal regulations.

The question of business ethics is of overriding concern to all public relations professionals working to achieve public acceptance and public support for the organizations that are their employers or clients. This fact is implicit in the view that public relations should be, *inter alia*, the conscience of the organization.

There have been a number of well publicized scandals recently in financial circles in the US, UK and Japan which have cast doubts on the integrity of business, but the majority of companies are very jealous of their reputation and take great care to protect it from any criticism. The

Vauxhall Motor Company, for example, follows General Motors' policy and does not allow any employee to accept a gift of any kind worth more than $25. Similar policies are operated by many other large companies.

Ethics are established by what a company does, not by what it says. It is necessary to act in a way that serves, and is seen to be serving the public good. Ethical and moral values are not absolute and their articulation in any organization will be culture bound but not influenced by strategic or tactical policies. The public relations associations and the professional press have been devoting increased attention to ethical values. The International Public Relations Association (IPRA) published in 1991 a monograph on *Ethical dilemmas in public relations — a pragmatic examination* which discusses some of the ethical issues that arise and the grey areas that present so many problems. In 1991 the Public Relations Society of America (PRSA) devoted its annual conference to an in-depth examination of ethical principles under the title: 'What's right?'

The Codes of Professional Conduct of the national public relations associations give guidance to practitioners but however detailed the recommendations, there will always be ethical issues which are not covered by the rule book. Three American professors, who have written extensively on this subject have made a number of comments which are worth noting.

Professor Frank Wylie, of California State University, has pointed out that there are two major components in business ethics:[*]

1. The responsibility of performing one's duties in an ethical manner.
2. The responsibility of performing one's duties in a capable manner.

Wylie comments that such a combination will not guarantee a desired level of excellence but rather a minimally acceptable level of performance. He suggests that there are important similarities in the behaviour of 'moral man' and the experienced pragmatist. While the moral man acts from belief in ethical behaviour, the experienced pragmatist adopts a pattern of behaviour because experience has proven that it is the best, or least dangerous course of action. Therefore whether one adopts a moral or a pragmatic point of view the behaviour is often the same.

Professor Melvin Sharpe, of Ball State University, Muncie, Indiana has been searching the literature for apposite arguments and has found the following[**]:

■ Decisions made in backrooms, even though ethically derived, carry the taint of distrust. Reality and image must mesh; justice must not only be done, it must be seen to be done.

---

[*] Wylie, Frank (1991) *Public Relations Quarterly*, Summer, pp. 7-13
[**] Sharpe, Melvin (1990) *International Public Relations Review, vol.13 no.3 pp.21-5*

- Confucius saw 'reciprocity' as the most important principle to follow in the conduct of life.
- Spinoza saw that self-preservation called for the necessity of a genuine concern for the well-being of others.
- Erich Fromm, in his writings, calls the 'fairness' concept the capitalist system's 'greatest gift to the world — the concept that I give you in goods and services equal to what you give me'.

Sharpe suggests the following as the ethical goal for those engaged in public relations:

- Ensure the organization communicates honestly — so that it will have credibility.
- Ensure the organization is open and consistent in all its actions — so that it will have public confidence.
- Ensure the organization evaluates the fairness of its actions — so that it will receive fair treatment.
- Ensure the organization maintains continuous communication — so that there can be mutual understanding and respect.
- Ensure the organization accurately researches its social environment — so that it can communicate its positions more effectively and change its actions when they are no longer serving the public interest.

Professor Donald K Wright, of South Alabama University,* has insisted that the study of public relations ethics must be more situational than theoretical. He comments that the operation of ethics today is an important consideration for the concerned, contemporary professional communicator, and in both simple and complex ways, public relations practitioners throughout the world are held together by a commonly held sense of necessary professional ethical conduct reinforced by accepted codes of professional conduct.

Wright comments that in the light of the complexity and nature of public relations, modern social psychology theory is not as germane to discussions of ethical development in this field as is the Socratic viewpoint. Some might consider it paradoxical that in a field founded firmly on modern social science and behavioural principles, the most relevant source for this study is not Sigmund Freud but Socrates, the ancient believer in the ideal form of the good. Yet contemporary scholars in other disciplines also have realized increasingly that morality and ethical development are reasserted more by the Socratic faith in the power of the rational good than by any other philosophical theory.

Chester Burger, a well-known New York consultant, has suggested that when we talk about ethics, we rarely consider the problems of the real

---

* Wright, Donald (1982) *Public Relations Journal,* December, pp.12-16

world.[†] He has stated that in more than 40 years working in the communications field he has learnt four important lessons:

Lesson 1: Communicators must trust the common sense of their audience. More often than not, the public will justify our trust by seeing accurately the issues and the contenders and the motivations. Communicators should not use clever headlines, gimmicks, distortions or lies to communicate effectively. It is a mistake to underestimate the public's perceptiveness.

Lesson 2: People generally will know or care very little about the issue that concerns you. It is necessary to inform, to clarify and simplify issues in a truthful manner in ways that will relate to the self-interest of the audience.

Lesson 3: Never compromise your own ethical standards for anyone. Do not say what you do not really believe and never do, for the sake of expediency, what you think is wrong.

Lesson 4: Choices for communicators between right and wrong are rarely *yes* or *no*. Questions of ethics often involve degrees, nuances and differing viewpoints. A little uncertainty and humility sometimes is approriate in considering ethical questions.

Principles of ethical power

The five 'Ps of ethical power' — Purpose, Pride, Patience, Persistence and Perspective (see Figures 13.1 and 13.2) are described and advocated by Kenneth Blanchard and Norman Vincent Peale in their book *The Power of Ethical Management* (William Heinemann, 1988) which has the racy sub-title 'you don't have to cheat to win'. These five broad principles of ethical behaviour are an excellent guide for public relations practitioners and other professionals.

The same book suggests an ethics checklist:

1. Is it legal? — will I be violating either civil law or company policy?
2. Is it balanced? — is it fair to all concerned in the short term as well as the long term? Does it promote win-win relationships?
3. How will it make me feel about myself? — Would I feel good if my decision was published in the newspaper?

---

† Burger, Chester (1982) *Public Relations Journal*, December, pp.13-17

The 'Five Ps'

1. **Purpose:** The mission of our organization is communicated from the top. Our organization is guided by the values, hopes, and a vision that helps us to determine what is acceptable and unacceptable behavior.

2. **Pride:** We feel proud of ourselves and of our organization. We know that when we feel this way, we can resist temptations to behave unethically.

3. **Patience:** We believe that holding to our ethical values will lead us to success in the long term. This involves maintaining a balance between obtaining results and caring how we achieve these results.

4. **Persistence:** We have a commitment to live by ethical principles. We are committed to our commitment. We make sure our actions are consistent with our purpose.

5. **Perspective:** Our managers and employees take time to pause and reflect, take stock of where we are, evaluate where we are going and determine how we are going to get there.

Figure 13.1 *The five principles of ethical power for organizations*

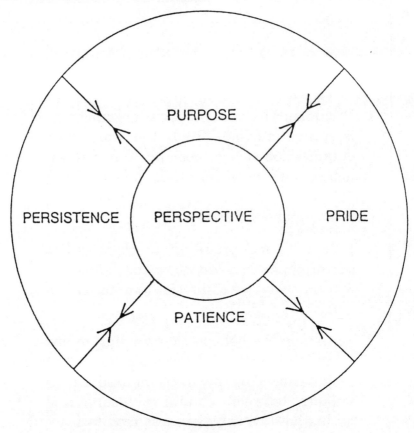

Figure 13.2 *The interrelationship between the five Ps*

A Rotary viewpoint

The *Four Way Test*, developed by Rotary International and which is binding on all Rotarians, asks four simple questions: Is it the truth? Is it fair to all concerned? Will it build goodwill and better friendship? Will it be beneficial to all concerned?

Development of ethical codes

The Code of Professional Conduct of the Institute of Public Relations is binding on all members of the Institute. The code lays down in detail the guidelines to which members should adhere in their relations with the public, the media and other professionals. It also describes correct conduct in relationships with employers and clients. The following extracts from the code are reprinted here by permission of the Institute:

1.1 A member shall have a positive duty to observe the highest standards in the practice of public relations and to deal fairly and honestly with employers and clients (past and present), fellow members and professionals, the public relations profession, other professions, suppliers, intermediaries, the media of communications, employers and the public.

1.4 A member shall not engage in any practice nor be seen to conduct him or herself in any manner detrimental to the reputation of the Institute or the reputation and interests of the public relations profession.

2.1 A member shall conduct his or her professional activities with proper regard to the public interest.

2.3 A member shall have a duty to ensure that the actual interest of any organization with which he or she may be professionally concerned is adequately declared.

2.6 A member shall ensure that the names of all directors, executives and retained advisers of his or her employers or company who hold public office as members of either House of Parliament, Local Authorities or other statutory organization or body are recorded in the IPR Register.

2.8 A member shall neither propose nor undertake any action which would be an improper influence on government legislation, holders of public office or members of any statutory body or organization, or the media of communication.

3.1 A member shall safeguard the confidences of both present and former employers or clients, shall not disclose or use these confidences to the disadvantage or prejudice of such employers or clients, or to the financial advantage of the member (unless the employer or client has released such information for public use, or has given specific permission for disclosure) except upon the order of a court of law.

3.5 A member shall not misuse information regarding his or her employer's or clients' business for financial or other gain.

3.6 A member shall not use inside information for gain. Nor may a member of staff managed or employed by a member directly trade in his or her employer's or client's securities without the prior written permission of the employer or client and of the member's chief executive or chief financial officer or compliance officer.

3.8 A member shall not represent conflicting interests but may represent competing interests with the express consent of the parties concerned.

3.9 A member shall not guarantee the achievement of results which are beyond the member's direct capacity to achieve or prevent.

4.1 A member shall adhere to the highest standards of accuracy and truth, avoiding extravagant claims or unfair comparisons and giving credit for ideas and words borrowed from others.

4.3 A member shall not injure the professional reputation or practice of another member.

The full text of the IPR Code of Professional Conduct, together with explanatory notes, can be obtained from the Institute of Public Relations,

15 Northburgh Street, London EC1V 0PR. In the interpretation attached to the code for the guidance of members, the Institute comments that the code is not a piece of window dressing; members have a positive duty to observe it.

Since the code was adopted by the Institute in 1963, there have been a number of complaints against members, serious and trivial, and in some instances the member concerned has been expelled from membership. The weakness of this disciplinary procedure is that expulsion from the Institute does not, in itself, prevent a practitioner from continuing in practice. Nevertheless, the terms of the code are an excellent guide to correct behaviour and few people would wish to be declared publicly to have contravened it. There is also the loss of ability to use the Institute's endorsement.

There is also a European Code of Professional Conduct (the Code of Lisbon) and an IPRA Code of Professional Conduct. Both these codes are similar to the IPR Code but are adapted to meet European or international situations. Both the European Public Relations Confederation (CERP) and the International Public Relations Association expect their members also to adhere to the Code of Athens. This is a code of morals and ethics based on the United Nations Declaration of Human Rights.

The Institute of Chartered Secretaries and Administrators (ICSA) has recently reminded its members of the importance of observing the Institute's strict code of professional conduct. The Institute has stated publicly that members who abide by the ICSA code will be able to rely on the support of the Institute if this brings them into conflict with their employers. The exact nature of this 'support' will presumably be established by case law. This practical approach could well be emulated by other professional bodies.

Another noteworthy development in this field has been the announcement that the Manchester Business School has appointed Brian Harvey as a professor of corporate social responsibility. He has been reported as planning to research the possible relationship between corporate responsibility and corporate success.

Conclusion

Ethical intentions, as expressed in mission statements or codes of conduct, must be backed up by positive action to ensure that these values are understood and accepted throughout the organization. Codes of conduct are excellent guides to correct behaviour but their value lies in strict adherence to both their letter and spirit.

14

International public relations and networking

The usual definition of international public relations is: the attempt to achieve mutual understanding by bridging a geographical, cultural or linguistic gap — or all of these at the same time. The term is also used to denote public relations activities which are carried out or have a positive significance outside the country of origin.

Successive public relations world congresses have emphasized the growing development of the interdependent world. New developments in science and technology, and the growing sophistication of computer software, combined with the ready availability of satellite communication, have certainly brought countries closer together.

Public relations tries to achieve harmony and understanding and the avoidance of conflict. It is about reputation, accountability, credibility and confidence. It is important to remember that these considerations have a universal application. The philosophy of public relations is very similar in all the different countries of the world, but the actual planning and operation of programmes must take into account culture, religion, traditions, economic conditions and other aspects of value judgments. For these reasons of cultural differences, it has become accepted that a large multinational company can plan its public relations strategy and policy at headquarters but the programmes may have to be adapted to local conditions and needs. This concept has been enshrined in the slogan: 'think globally but act locally'. Dupont expresses it slightly differently: 'take a global view but village action'. (See case history later in this chapter.)

Possible pitfalls due to language differences

Apart from cultural differences, there are many examples of amusing but significant mistakes in marketing which could be parallelled in public relations programmes carried out from a distance in ignorance of the local language. A car that did not sell in one country because its name when translated meant 'coffin'. The deodorant commercial which, when shown in parts of Africa, suggested that women aggressively pursued the men, a practice bizarre in those cultures. The airline which produced a commercial promoting its 'rendezvous' lounges in Brazil only to learn that in Portuguese 'rendezvous' means 'a place to have sex'. Or the advertisements with the liberal use of white displayed, in countries where that colour is the symbol of death. These examples are not new, but they do show the kinds of serious errors that can occur in trying to design messages for other cultures or countries.

Non-verbal communication

In addition to language pitfalls, non-verbal communication, often referred to as body language, can sometimes give offence. A few years ago, the BAA ran a very amusing advertising campaign based on the fact that gestures and involuntary movements that are unnoticed in one country may give serious offence in others. It is possible to identify four different categories of non-verbal communication:

1. Symbolic gestures, such as a salute or thumbs up.
2. Emphasis while speaking, such as arms waving or pointing.
3. Facial movements indicating emotion, such as a smile, a grin or a grimace.
4. Nervous reactions, usually indicating anxiety or stress, such as fidgeting or swaying backwards and forwards.

Sometimes it is helpful to use some of these gestures, but unless their use is strictly controlled their effect may be counter productive. Similarly, posture can indicate emotional and mental states and attitudes to others. Cultural differences arise also from choice of clothes and the way they are worn.

Ethical considerations

In all relationships, commercial and non-commercial, it is essential to remember the importance of moral and ethical considerations. This is a basic and fundamental teaching of public relations which is of paramount importance in international public relations, just as it is in national or local circumstances.

Methods of organizing public relations internationally

A transnational corporation, with subsidiary companies in major areas of the world, may wish to keep public relations within its own branch offices.

This will mean that non-professional managers will have to deal with routine public relations requirements. If this is the choice of a large company it will be essential to provide regular guidance and supervision to reduce the possibility of ineptitude or inefficiency.

It is likely that the parent company will issue a Company Area Manager's Guide. A typical guide gave the following briefing:

> Our objective is to have all people who come into contact with our company regard it as a good company to work for, a good company to invest in, a good company to buy from, a good company to sell to, and a good company to have in any community.
>
> We want the public to know the company not only as an efficient, economic organization that designs, manufactures and sells products at a fair price, but also as a useful and desirable institution, recognizing and meeting its responsibilities to all groups that it serves.

This guide included the Institute of Public Relations' definition of public relations and suggested good introductory textbooks.

Another method is to buy in public relations services, either on a continuing basis or as required. There are five different ways in which this can be organized:

1. There are a number of large public relations consultancies with branch offices in all the leading national commercial centres. These local offices have usually been established by the parent company and bear its name.
2. Another world-wide grouping has been built up by acquisition and the local name and staff is retained.
3. A form of networking has developed in which the leading member of the network takes an equity interest in agencies in many other countries.
4. Another type of networking, which has grown rapidly, consists of a number of prominent independent agencies, in different countries, retaining ownership of their own companies while enjoying the benefits of international affiliation. These networks usually have at least one regular annual meeting. A recent report in *PR Week* has given details of 10 European networks comprising agencies from Britain, Austria, Belgium, France, Germany, Italy and Spain which have become affiliated in the expectation of increased cross frontier opportunities from 1993.
5. A loose association of public relations agencies, which work together from time to time but have no regular meetings. Initial contact between these agencies probably resulted from their principals being members of the International Public Relations Association.

The ultimate justification of any of these methods is whether they can provide a very high level of professional service to clients on a local level while enjoying the support and sophisticated back-up of their network colleagues or parent organization.

Ellis Kopel, a well known international public relations expert, tells a true story which perhaps helps to put this whole subject into a proper perspective. His agency in London had as a client for ten years the cake and biscuit industries trade federation. When it first came up, his company was one of six consultancies selected to pitch for the business and one requirement was to demonstrate ability to work internationally. Having won the account, Kopel held it for ten years until the body amalgamated with another one. In all that time, no work outside Britain was required from his consultancy.

Media of communication

When media lists are drawn up locally the normal choice applies, but when trying to carry out media relations from a distance it may be necessary to rely more on the increasing number of international business newspapers. The *Financial Times* now has 20 fully manned bureaux overseas and international editions are printed in the US, Germany, France and Japan. This edition claims a circulation of over 100,000 copies. The European edition of *The Wall Street Journal* is now selling over 50,000 copies and its Asian edition is selling about 40 000. There is also the *International Herald Tribune* which circulates widely. Whether it is better to use these international media or to concentrate on local and national media will depend on the objectives. In dealing with national and local media, the importance of knowing local customs and traditions in either case is paramount. Methods which are quite acceptable in some countries are out of order in others.

Case history 21
Global view and village action — Du Pont

The E. I. Du Pont Nemours Company Inc can truly claim to be a global company as it operates in 54 countries. Its presence in Asia/Pacific is relatively small but the company is determined to grow in the region. The growth strategy is to build product resources near its potential customers and Du Pont has begun or will begin production at 18 new plants in Asia/ Pacific.

In the course of this substantial expansion in the region, Du Pont has learnt the importance of understanding the needs of the local customers and communities where they seek to do business. Du Pont has four primary constituencies: employees, customers, shareholders and society. The company now realizes that 'consent to operate' from local communities is essential. It is imperative to be viewed and to act as a local, committed company.

A tale of three plants in Taiwan
Chungli
Chungli, near Taipei, opened in 1970 and reached a peak employment of 1100 in 1984. The plant was producing mainly for the US electronic markets and as the demand dropped, more than 600 employees had been shed by 1987.

The easy solution would have been to close the plant. Under excellent leadership from the local Chinese management, however, the Chungli employees directed their efforts to meet the needs of local Taiwan customers. This has proved very successful and the future of the factory is assured. Du Pont learnt from this experience that businesses are best managed by developing key local leaders and letting them meet local conditions.

Lungtan
Lungtan was opened in 1980 and produces Du Pont chemicals for use in the protection of agricultural products. The employees created their own teamwork system long before it became a popular concept. The plant has real customer focus and produces agrochemicals designed for the unique soil and climate conditions found in each area of Taiwan. Lungtan employees live in the 'village' with their customers, the farmers, and so are able to respond quickly to their particular needs.

Kuan Yin
The reality at Kuan Yin, now under construction, had shown a very different series of events. When it opens in 1993, the factory will produce titanium dioxide, a non-toxic pigment that enhances the colour of paints, plastics, textiles and even toothpaste and cake frosting.

Du Pont have no doubt of the safety of titanium dioxide production. Similar plants operate in the local community at Du Pont world-wide headquarters in Wilmington, Delaware in the USA. The fact that the plant would be safe and environmentally sound was not believed by the local community at Kuan Yin and this disquiet and subsequent protests delayed the whole project three years. The difficulties arose from a lack of communication and prior discussion with the local community. It emphasizes, once again, the importance of valuing the experience and knowledge of local employees and taking them into the company's confidence at an early stage and before final plans are settled.

The company's experience at these three different sites has convinced them of the need to value village action which must be balanced by the company's global policy and strategy.

Du Pont believe they have learnt four lessons from their experiences in Taiwan:

1. Global networks allow for technology transfer and early warning of global trends.

2. Forward planning must take into account the needs of local customers and communities.
3. Give opportunities to local people so that they can develop their management potentialities.
4. It is essential to appreciate the continuing and developing needs of customers and communities.

Summary
Taking the term 'global village' from Marshall McLuhan, Du Pont Public Affairs Department has adopted the slogan: 'Global view and village action'. They have found this philosophy works very well in the Asia/Pacific region and is probably equally valid world-wide.

Comment
The experience of Du Pont at Kuan Yin emphasizes the validity of the public relations teaching that it is essential to forestall opposition by early and comprehensive adequate local consultation. Carried out successfully, this gives the local community a personal stake in the progress of the enterprise which they begin to regard as their own project.

Case history 22
Bringing satellite communication to Armenia — AT & T

The world is carrying out a staggering amount of telecommunication these days, but capabilities are far from evenly distributed round the world. There are about 500 million telephone exchange lines in the world. Of these, the US has about 120 million and Japan has more than 50 million. In terms of telephone lines per 100 people, Sweden leads with 65.

The world's telephones make more than 700 billion calls each year. Only a small percentage of these calls are between different countries, but they add up to about 10 billion minutes of international calling. These voice, data, fax and video signals travel over about 170 communications satellites, 78 000 km of underwater fibre optic cable and an almost infinite length of land-based cable. The degree of access to this multifaceted world-wide network has much to do with people's expectations.

In the Republic of Armenia, A T & T's Public Relations Division has had an unusually interesting experience, the impact of which leaped an ocean and two continents — from Yerevan to New York and Los Angeles — by confounding expectations in all these places.

Linking Armenia with the USA
The installation of an A T & T international gateway switch and a satellite earth station last year made Armenia the first former Soviet republic, other than Russia, to have a direct telecommunications link to the USA. These 180 new satellite circuits represented an enormous emotional leap for Armenians and for the approximately one million ethnic Armenians who live in the US. This Armenian community is tight-knit and remains committed to the homeland, despite having little opportunity to communicate with loved ones there.

Telecom modernization promised opportunities for economic development and renewed family ties. This was taking place after the coup but
before the final dissolution of the Soviet empire, so the new telecommunications system also meant a measure of insurance that newly-won freedoms
would not be easily snatched away — least not without the world knowing.

The public relations plan for celebrating this auspicious occasion
included an Armenian style barbecue beneath the huge satellite dish for
about 200 officials, media representatives and A T & T executives. Guests
and reporters from outside Yerevan would never consider taking commercial flights there for fear of being stranded by fuel shortages, so a special
flight had to be chartered from Moscow. Negotiations for fuel supplies
continued right up to the last minute. It was arranged for toilets to be shipped
from the Netherlands for installation in the ill-equipped Ministry of Communications building. Unfortunately, the precious porcelains disappeared
in transit and have not been seen since. It was also planned for the event to
be linked by conference call to New York and Los Angeles. In New York,
600 Armenian church, academic, business and community leaders and
ranking envoys were to have breakfast with a senior AT&T officer. In Los
Angeles, the star of the show was the Armenian Minister of Culture, a
successful author who happened to be in the US, participating in an AT&T
sponsored international writers programme. He hosted a group of school-
children of Armenian descent who had created artwork to be faxed to
Yerevan during the ceremony.

So it was at 4 pm Yerevan time, 9 am in New York and a sleepy 6 am in
Los Angeles that the call went through. Few public relations events have
had such an emotional reception. Participants at all locations burst into
joyful applause. Armenian officials introduced the Republic's first postage
stamp since the 1920s; it combined the icons of Mount Ararat, a satellite
dish and the AT&T name. The Armenian caterer in New York, a shrewd
negotiator who had driven a tough bargain, was so moved that he suddenly
declared the food to be his gift. Finally, the Armenian Orthodox bishop
blessed AT&T and all its people. When was the last time that an Orthodox
bishop blessed a multinational company?

Masses of media coverage was achieved in the targeted media,
especially in Armenia, Russia, the Netherlands and the US. All this publicity
had enormous impact on call volumes from the US to Armenia. From all
perspectives, this unusual event was a big success. Although AT&T install
many switches in many countries, few get this kind of attention — but then
few countries go, like Armenia, in one leap from virtual isolation to become
part of the world-wide telecommunications network.

Comment
This interesting AT & T case history illustrates how a normal technical
event, opening a new telecommunications link, can with imagination and
creativity be used to engender a remarkable level of goodwill, as well as
increased business for the company.

Case history 23
Informing a multicultural community at the Hague

This is an account of international community relations activities in Greater Hague, in the Netherlands, one of the most densely populated, multi-ethnic areas in Western Europe. It was carried out for the Hague Municipality by Dora Molleson. an independent public relations consultant, who was previously in charge of the foreign desk in the Hague Municipality's Information Department.

The rationale of the programme

According to the Civil Registry, nationals of more than 125 countries live and work in Greater Hague. A variety of programmes, sponsored by the local authority and semi-official organizations, aim at improving inter-communal relations by introducing to the foreign community the country, its people, its history and culture, as well as its economic and political aspects.

In addition to acting as guide and interpreter for official guests from Poland and Russia, Dora Molleson was mainly responsible for two community relations programmes: *Letter from the Hague* and a series of lectures. 'The Country We Live in'.

Letter from the Hague

This eight page A4 newsletter is published every two months in English and is circulated to the English speaking international community and multinational companies, the *Corps Diplomatique*, international organizations, the Nether-land England Society, the British Women's Club, schools and universities and many other organizations with wide political and scientific affiliations.

The Ministry of Foreign Affairs sends the 'letter' to all Dutch missions abroad and 250 copies of each issue are sent to former Hague residents now living abroad. One hundred copies are sent to Ottawa, the Hague's twin city in Canada, and to other towns. Furthermore, several hundred copies are distributed to visitors to the Municipal Information Centre. The publication covers a very wide field likely to be of interest to four main categories of foreigners: temporary residents (on business or diplomats); mixed marriages; students from many different countries and the foreign press corps. Each issue carries an article based on an anniversary of historic importance. Topical subjects are included, such as the inauguration of the Parliamentary session, political summit meetings, royal or head of state visits and similar occasions. Once a year, there is a special feature on education based on a visit to one of the six foreign schools in the Hague (American, English, French, German and Indonesian).

Ideas and material for features in the issues are obtained by studying audio-visual presentations and documents in the Municipal Information Centre, visiting important exhibitions, interviews with public figures and officials, studying radio and press releases and attending some municipal council meetings which are open to the public. Other materials result from visits to municipal utilities: power generation, district heating or water treatment. The numerous cultural events in the Hague also produce reports and comments.

All items are discussed with officials or outside experts and the drafts are shown to the head of the Public Relations Department. A graphic artist helps with the layout which always includes diagrams or pictures.

'The Country We Live In'
This is an annual series of public lectures in English, followed by discussion. The series was initiated and run in cooperation with the Hague Cultural Centre, a public body concerned with adult education. The programme varies each year with speakers nominated by the Cultural Centre. They include politicians, artists, historians and journalists. The 1992 programme was the 36th season of the series, which has been held regularly by the Municipality since 1955.

The Municipality provides the venue and contributes a subsidy which meets about half the low admission fees. All the meetings are well attended and the positive reaction of the public has encouraged the continuation of this popular community project.

Comment
These two public relations programmes are among a very comprehensive menu of activities which demonstrate the Municipality's commitment to keeping its foreign guests informed.

Case history 24
International pen-friends

The pen-friend concept has been very popular in Europe for many years, encouraged by schools in many different countries. The friendships thus achieved have helped to spread a better understanding of how people live in other countries. A surprising number of pen-friends finish up marrying each other and while no statistics exist, it is safe to assume that these marriages are no less happy than those resulting from more conventional meetings.

The fascination of Americans with the international scene has increased dramatically during the last few years, fanned by a number of tumultuous world events. A Gallop poll in 1989 indicated that the last decade has witnessed a remarkable shift in Americans' perception about many foreign countries. A national poll in December 1990 of 1000 American households taken by National Family Opinion on behalf of American Greetings showed that:

1. 88 per cent of Americans believe a better understanding of other countries is a way to enhance world peace;
2. 89 per cent agreed that recent historical events have increased their interest in international affairs;
3. 33 per cent wanted to write to people overseas.

Advised by Edelman Public Relations, American Greetings, of Cleveland, Ohio, decided to satisfy this identified Americans' wish to communicate with people overseas and with the assistance of the consultancy an ambitious programme was produced to satisfy this desire. In addition to showing its interest in corporate social responsibility, the company wished to achieve four main commercial objectives:

- to confirm American Greetings as a leader in their field;
- to reinforce the company as a good corporate citizen;
- to support their retailers;
- to target the programme at their prime market, men and women aged between 18 and 49.

An 18 month campaign was launched with the slogan: 'American greetings to the world' and an International Pen Friend Network was established to match Americans with overseas pen pals by country, age and sex. Membership was free and included receipt of a specially prepared international correspondence guide.

The Network was established initially with the help of embassies, consulates and global pen-friend organizations to establish a database of international names. The consultancy then worked out a system for matching suitable pen-friends. The cooperation of the United Nations was readily forthcoming since the programme was likely to enhance world peace and harmony through intercultural education. The launch of the programme was held at UN Headquarters in New York. This was a most successful event which achieved much media attention and included the joint signing of a giant greeting card by a top Soviet general and a retired US Air Force General in the presence of children from the United Nations School. A nationwide contest to increase interest in international pen pals, co-sponsored by *Good Housekeeping*, sent one grand prize-winner to The Netherlands in Spring 1992 to meet her Russian pen-friend.

The results surpassed expectations. More than 560,000 Americans joined the network. More than 400 million consumers were reached by this scheme and 30,000 retailers reported increased sales.

The 'American greetings to the world' programme touched the pulse of the American public and opened numerous new lines of communications between the countries of the world. A New Orleans woman wrote that she had always wanted to join a pen pal organization but could not afford it. A Detroit woman informed them that she plans to marry her pen-friend from Morocco. A Russian man wrote . . . 'so significant a work you are doing excites nothing but admiration'.

In view of the remarkable success of this pilot scheme, American Greetings is sponsoring another national programme in 1992 and this may well become an annual programme.

Comment
This is another informative example of how it is possible to introduce a programme *pro bono publico* and at the same time produce substantial commercial benefit for the sponsoring organization.

The four short case histories in this chapter illustrate the very different types of public relations which can be regarded as 'international' in their objectives and performance.

15

A short history of the development of public relations practice

In considering the history of the profession, it is necessary to distinguish between the use of public relations as an integral part of government since the earliest days and the modern concept of public relations as a management discipline.

If we consider only one limited aspect of public relations, as persuasion directed at the public to modify attitudes and actions, it is possible to trace its use back to ancient Sumeria, Assyria, Persia and Egypt. There is ample evidence of persuasion being used to mould public opinion in the interests of the rulers. In ancient Greece and Rome this technique was highly developed and refined.

Dr Edward L Bernays, in his book *Public Relations* has traced the way in which public relations techniques were exploited through successive centuries and he quotes the French Revolution as a remarkable example of how the term 'public opinion' gained currency throughout Europe and the Americas.

In its Declaration of the Rights of Man, the French Revolution publicly proclaimed as one of the most important of these, the right to express and communicate thought freely. One of the most effective weapons of the Revolution was its handling of public relations. Every known weapon of word and deed was used to influence public opinion — books, pamphlets, newspaper, the stage, satire, hairdos, military insignia and cockades. Even clothes became symbols of ideas. Powdered wigs and knee breeches were discarded as they symbolized the old regime. Partisans wore their own hair and long trousers, which have remained part of modern Western man's costume.

It is possible to point to the influence of public relations in political and religious developments through the different historical periods. During the American Revolution, for example, the Declaration of Independence was a very powerful example. However, since this book is not a history, it is better to jump to more modern times and to quote 1923 as a suitable date to mark the start of 'professional' public relations. It was that year that Edward Bernays published his book *Crystallizing Public Opinion*. This book, published in New York, was the first textbook to describe public relations practice. Through widespread reviews of this book in the United States, thousands of people were exposed for the first time to the new concept of public relations. Many, however, still believed the term to be a euphemism for 'press agentry'.

Bernays realized that it would help to give the new term professional status if it was taught at a university. New York University agreed to allow him to teach a course on the principles, practice and ethics of public relations in 1923. This course was the forerunner of the many public relations programmes offered today in universities in the USA, Europe and many other countries.

Historical developments in Britain

In the United Kingdom, there were early isolated examples of the use of public relations in government circles. As early as 1809, the Treasury as the department of state chiefly concerned with the machinery of government, assumed the role of press spokesman on overseas policy. In 1912, Lloyd George, then Chancellor of the Exchequer, organized a corps of lecturers to explain the new National Insurance Act to employers and workers in many parts of the country.

The major impetus to the rapid development of public relations in the US and Britain came from the two world wars. This led to many young men and women gaining the opportunity of experience in this new activity. After World War 1, Bernays and others who had served on the USA Creel Committee brought their new skills to the service of American commerce and industry.

In Britain, many men and women who had, during World War 2, been doing public relations in the Armed Services and in the Ministry of Information, decided to make a career in this new vocation. With the encouragement of NALGO, the National Association of Local and Government Officers, local goverment became very interested and many councils appointed public relations officers.

Formation of the Institute of Public Relations

Practitioners working in local government began meeting together informally and the idea of establishing an association of public relations began to crystallize. Contact was made with Sir Stephen Tallents,

KCMG,CB,CBE, who had recently retired from Government service after a distinguished career in public relations, and he was asked if he would convene a meeting of people working in public relations in the Government and in industry to meet local government public relations officers. This meeting took place on 21 April 1947 when it was agreed that positive steps be taken to investigate the feasibility of joining together in a professional institute.

After further discussions between interested parties, the Institute of Public Relations (IPR) was formed at an inaugural meeting at St Bride's Institute in London on 10 February 1948. Sir Stephen Tallents was elected the first president, a position which he occupied again in 1952–53. His support and encouragement was invaluable in those early days.

The Institute has had a profound effect on the development of public relations practice in Britain and currently has a professional membership of over 4000. Full membership of the Institute now requires a recognized academic public relations qualification and four years' comprehensive practical experience. As early as 1951, the Institute issued advice to members on professional conduct and this was later developed into a very comprehensive Code of Professional Conduct to which all members must adhere.

Rather similar parallel developments have taken place in the United States and many other countries. National public relations institutes or associations have been formed and have been growing steadily in size and influence. The largest and most active is the Public Relations Society of America (PRSA) with a membership of over 15,000.

This rapid world-wide development has been encouraged and assisted by the formation in May, 1955 of the International Public Relations Association (IPRA). This body was formed initially by senior members of the profession from five countries: Britain. France, The Netherlands, Norway and the US. IPRA now has 1000 members from 64 countries. IPRA's main objectives are to promote public relations education and research, to encourage the highest possible standards of professional performance and ethics, and to develop a better understanding of the importance of the practice as a management discipline. It seeks to achieve its objectives through publications and research papers and by holding regional and world congresses.

IPRA is recognized by the United Nations as an International Non-governmental Organization for purposes of consultation. It also has Consultative Status, Category B with Unesco. In addition to professional considerations, the Association sets up special task forces to consider topical issues such as 'Public relations and the environment', 'The status of children', and 'Developments in Eastern Europe'.

A few examples will illustrate the spread of interest in public relations practice. New public relations associations have been formed in Hungary and Russia while China has established national public relations bodies. In Nigeria, government decree requires membership of the national institute as a requirement for those wishing to practise. In Spain, it is necessary to satisfy standards set out by the government in order to have a licence to practise as a public relations practitioner. Somewhat similar rules apply in Brazil. In most countries, however, the qualification requirements are established by the national public relations associations without govenmental involvement.

Public relations has become generally recognized and understood world-wide and it is now accepted as an important function of management and a useful contribution to running successfully and profitably any kind of company or organization.

16

Public relations education and career prospects

Business and management studies are becoming one of the fastest growing areas of higher education in Britain. During the last five years, undergraduate and postgraduate degrees in public relations have become established in the British university system. The first degree programme was the MSc in Public Relations at the University of Stirling in Scotland. The one year full-time masters programme at Stirling was introduced in 1978 and has attracted students from many parts of the world, with the majority of the students coming from the United Kingdom. The demand far outstrips the available number of places each year and there should be good prospects for the new postgraduate degree course at Manchester Metropolitan University.

A similar MSc in Public Relations has been introduced at Stirling on a three year distance learning basis and this too has proved very popular, with students coming from the UK and many overseas countries. This programme includes a compulsory one week residential course in each of the three years.

A one year postgraduate diploma course has been offered since 1987 by West Herts College at its Watford campus. This course, which has an international dimension, is sponsored by the Public Relations Consultants Association.

Several undergraduate degrees in public relations are now available in Britain. BA Hons degree programmes are offered by Bournemouth University, Leeds Metropolitan University and the College of St Mark and St John, Plymouth (University of Exeter). The demand for these courses continues to be very high, with as many as 20 eligible applicants for each available place.

The place of public relations in management education

Another recent development has been the introduction of public relations courses into management and business studies programmes at degree and HND levels. A number of business schools and university management departments have included public relations as an elective subject or an option. This is a welcome development as until recently MBA programmes completely ignored public relations or merely mentioned it as a minor aspect of marketing or advertising.

A research paper published in 1991 by the Public Relations Education Trust quoted the results of a questionnaire sent to the majority of colleges providing postgraduate management education in the United Kingdom. The most significant question asked: 'Do you agree that public relations is an important element in management?' Out of 54 completed questionnaires, only two replied 'no', 52 replied 'yes' to this fundamental question. Yet few colleges stated that public relations found a place in their core curriculum or even as an elective.

This paradoxical situation is slowly changing as deans of business schools and management colleges are realizing that as a management discipline of some importance, public relations should find a place in all management programmes.

A curriculum model

Few professions have rigidly standardized educational syllabuses but all have generally accepted educational standards and requirements. The International Public Relations Association (IPRA) has published two gold papers (in 1982 and 1990) setting out recommendations and standards which have been accepted internationally. In the United States, where public relations education has been established at many universities since 1923, the Public Relations Society of America (PRSA) has published a number of reports which are in general agreement with the IPRA recommendations.

Entrance to the profession comes at different levels. A student may take an undergraduate degree lasting three or four years full-time. A more mature person, with some years experience, can take a masters programme. Specialists coming from other professions will need a conversion syllabus. For managers who may be responsible for the overall utilization of public relations without being personally involved in its day-to-day operation, a general appreciation of the potential of public relations in management is all that is required and this should have been obtained previously as a part of general management training. The general concept of public relations education and training is similar to the training of a doctor. A student needs to cover a very wide field which leads to a general degree. Thereafter, he or she may wish to concentrate on one of the specialities such as financial public relations or parliamentary liaison.

The IPRA reports recommend a well-rounded education and training which includes the general liberal arts and humanities to which specific knowledge and experience in communication and public relations is added. This is illustrated in the Wheel of Education, Figure 16.1.

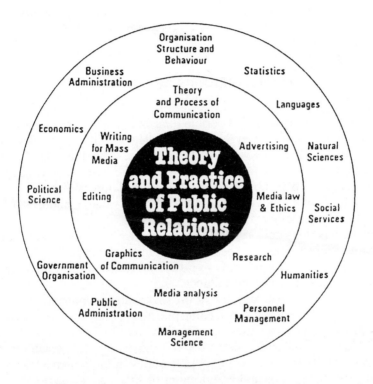

Figure 16.1 *The wheel of education according to IPRA*

The curriculum for a student wishing to enter the profession can be pictured as a series of three concentric circles. The smallest central circle encloses the subjects specifically concerned with public relations practice. The second, larger circle lists the subjects in the general field of communication. The third and largest circle represents the general liberal arts and humanities which are essential preparation for a successful professional. This model, first presented by IPRA in 1982, and elaborated in 1990, has been generally accepted but it leaves room for a certain degree of adaptation by colleges introducing new programmes or modifying existing ones. The MSc degree in public relations at the University of Stirling, mentioned earlier in this chapter, was based on

IPRA Gold Paper no. 4 on education and in 1992, the University of Nigeria introduced a MSc degree programme in public relations, based on IPRA Gold Papers nos 4 and 7.

Another interesting new development has been the introduction of a European MA degree programme in public relations. This is being offered jointly by universities in Britain, France, Belgium, Italy and Portugal.

The future development of public relations degree programmes is likely to be at national level but increasingly to embrace a more transnational character.

Public relations as a career

Dismay has been expressed in certain quarters over the growing number of men and women emerging from colleges with public relations qualifications. This fear is groundless as many people taking public relations courses regard them as an additional skill rather than necessarily as a means to practise public relations full-time. There is no doubt that an understanding of public relations can be of great value to people working in a wide range of other occupations.

The demand for public relations has been growing world-wide at a rate of about 25 per cent per year and, despite some cutbacks due to recessionary pressures, it is safe to forecast a continuing strong demand both in-house and in the consultancy field.

Some people express surprise at the increasing proportion of women entering the profession. Many senior positions are now held by women practitioners who have shown imagination and ability to succeed at the highest levels of the profession. Not all practitioners can reach the top, however, and there are excellent opportunities for both men and women at many different levels and in a number of specialities.

The financial rewards compare favourably with similar types of work. The Institute of Public Relations publishes details from time to time of the average remuneration of its members and these have shown a steady increase.

Public relations is not an easy job. Success demands many attributes, including common sense, curiosity, ability to communicate orally and in writing, flexibility, stamina, attention to detail, a good general education and an ability to cope with concentrated effort when required. Liking people is not essential, but it helps. Understanding people and their likes and dislike is even more valuable.

Further reading

There are many good books available which would amplify this text. The following list is a representative selection.

Black, Sam (1989) *Introduction to Public Relations*, Modino, London.
Black, Sam (1989) *Exhibitions and Conferences from A to Z*, Modino, London.
Black, Sam (ed.) (1993) *International Public Relations Case Studies*, Kogan Page, London.
Ellis, Nigel (1988) *Parliamentary Lobbying*, Heinemann, Oxford.
Ind, Nicholas (1991) *The Corporate Image*, Kogan Page, London.
Moss, Danny (ed.) (1990) *Public Relations Practice — a Casebook*, Routledge, London.
Nally, Margaret (ed.) (1992) *International Public Relations in Practice*, Kogan Page, London.
Regester, Michael (1989) *Crisis Management — how to turn a crisis into an opportunity*, Hutchinson Business, London.
Ryder, Neil and Regester, Michael (1990) *Investor Relations*, Hutchinson Business, London.
Stone, Norman (1991) *How to Manage Public Relations*, McGraw-Hill, Maidenhead.
White, Jon (1991) *How to Understand and Manage Public Relations*, Business Books, London.

Index